Taranaki Sunshine

Tales from an Okoki Childhood

Sonya Vince

Copyright 2016: Sonya Vince

All rights reserved. Without limiting the rights under copyright reserved above, no part of this work/publication may be reproduced, stored in or introduced into a retrieval system, or transmitted, in any form or by any means (electronic, mechanical, print, photocopying, recording or otherwise), without the prior written permission of the copyright owner.

ISBN: 978-0-6484077-1-3

Nonfiction/memoir

Taranaki Sunshine is a combination of fiction and nonfiction. Many of the stories are fictitious, with any resemblance to any person, living or deceased, being coincidental. Where the stories are based on fact names and places may have been changed, and some minor facts altered to protect others. Every attempt has been made to give appropriate acknowledgment for material, visual or written.

Dedication

To Ian, who has for a number of years, said with totally biased admiration "You should write a book."

And to Mary and Linda who made me do it.

Contents

An Okoki Childhood 1
A Child of The World 3
The Great Okoki Floods 6
Country Folk 10
Sundry Pets 14
Farm Dogs 19
Eels 22
Pot of Gold 25
Dreaming Through Childhood 29
Worlds of Imagination 34
Easter 37
Winter Warmth 39
The Fireplace 42
Rain on the Roof 47
Calf Judging Day 49
Chamber Secrets 53
Potato Stamp Redemption 56
What Rosie Saw 60
Winners & Losers 63
Blue Satin Dress 66
On the Bus 70
After School Adventures 74
Nights on the Front Verandah 78
An Okoki Christmas 81
Mum's Christmas Cake 87

Backstage on Christmas Day 88
Memories in a Blackberry Jam Jar 93
Food Fit for Children, & Pigs 96
Cooked Watercress 97
Bread and milk 97
Jerusalem Artichokes 98
Yeast Drinks 98
Junket 98
The Dromorne Linen Man 100
My Paternal Grandmother 105
Doors & Scents 106
Funeral 108
Farm Life & Death 112
Time Warp 118
Pants on fire 125
The Interview 128
Red Dress 131
Photos From Our Album 139
The Weed in The Garden 144
Acknowledgements 145

An Okoki Childhood

In these pages I look back on the life of a small, scrawny, restless child, as if I were seeing someone I haven't met or known previously.

I invite you to come with me as I return, often as "Rosie", to Okoki—my home and my childhood world.

"Okoki, where's that?" queries someone from Taranaki, let alone the rest of New Zealand. Chances are they've never heard of this isolated little no-exit valley whose closest hamlet is Urenui, and whose nearest town, Waitara, is 32 miles away.

In the Forties and Fifties the roads were 'rough as guts' and the drive from Okoki to New Plymouth in our 1934 pre-Holden, mud-coloured Chevy took a good hour each way. A family shopping excursion to the 'city' was a full-day affair, and done only infrequently.

In those days self-sufficiency was not simply a lifestyle choice or a virtue—it was a near necessity.

I have no idea how the term 'Taranaki Sunshine' originated, but it was our ironic term for rain, falling as the sun shone—those showers when the wind blew the clouds aside and the sun gave raindrops a transparent, golden glow.

We parroted "Taranaki Sunshine!" as we looked out of school windows on wet days. Because our farming economy depended upon a high rainfall, we accepted damp weather without dismay even though torrential downpours flooded the valley to alarming levels with some regularity.

These mysterious showers stopped as quickly as they began and were always welcome. We loved these magical showers. To a child, they meant drama and adventure.

We truly loved our Taranaki Sunshine.

A Child of The World

Sonya Ekdahl
Piko Road
Okoki
Urenui
Taranaki
North Island
New Zealand
Pacific Ocean
Southern Hemisphere
The World.
The Universe

This crudely pencilled inscription is on the flyleaf of a small red-covered edition of Blackie's School Dictionary, an unlikely survivor of my school days.

Although I acknowledged my citizenship of Universe and World, my knowledge of it was limited to the first 4 entries.

It seems I was meant to have my place in the scheme of things, in spite of the fact that it took six years and many of my mother's prayers for my parents to conceive me.

Three times in the years before I was old enough to recall, my life was nearly claimed.

At the age of six weeks, I contracted the dreaded whooping cough. Neighbours who had the scourge came visiting the new and long awaited baby. Shortly after I was in a life-threatening situation, whooping and gasping. My parents took me into town to the Doctor. My desperate mother told him she'd heard that garlic rubbed on the soles of little feet would help.

The doctor looked at my mother, took her hands gently in his and replied "My dear, anything you might want to do for this baby, just go ahead and try. Anything." He didn't expect me to live.

Maybe it was the garlic, and maybe it was more of my dear mother's prayers, because I survived six weeks of the drastic illness, emerging thin as a slabby trout, with legs like Manuka pea sticks.

At about three years of age I was nearly exported to Britain in a bale of wool. My parents noticed I was missing one day during shearing time when the shearers were about to press another wool bail. Adjoining sacks were filled with fleeces by the Fleece-O. With the aid of a winch wheel, one bale of wool was hoisted up and pressed down into the other. While the press was in place the two bails were sewed together. When the press was released, the door opened and out bounced a tightly filled bail of wool, ready for stencilling our trade name and details, and trucked to the Wanganui Wool Sales.

My father would not allow the shearers to proceed with the pressing until everyone had searched some more. Someone had already checked to see if I was up in the wool bail but my thorough and anxious father searched there himself.

He found me almost completely obscured by fleeces as I lay there sound asleep, no doubt lulled off by the hum of the machinery, the warmth of the shed and the softness of the wool.

The third drama took place, while my mother and older sister were bathing in a deep pool in the creek. Somehow I fell into the water and was gone without a trace.

The tannin-stained water made it quite impossible to see below the surface. Desperately my mother dived again and again and found me, pulled me to the surface. She shook the water out of my lungs by holding me upside down by my ankles.

After my three tribulations it seemed I was destined to live.

They were by no means the last of my perils and mishaps. On our remote and hilly farm and in the days before Occupational Health & Safety, there were always elements of danger.

My earliest memory was one of a more minor disaster. A much older cousin had been doubling me on a newly acquired bicycle, a vehicle of rarity in the Valley in those days.

I failed to hold my legs out clear of the wheel spokes and had the skin dramatically barked off one ankle. I recall being held aloft, with what seemed oceans of blood, howling lustily.

The Great Okoki Floods

An Okoki flood brought danger, excitement, and not a little diversion from the routine of farm life. As children we adored floods—the bigger the better.

The violent upheavals of the 1942 flood permanently altered Okoki. The uprooted trees, massive boulders relocated, and damaged bridges were just some of the effects of the deluge. My oldest sister is shown here, surveying the scene.

Spring floods were memorable. With an annual rainfall measured in feet, the dark tannin-stained creeks burst into raging, coffee-coloured torrents several times each year. But all floods in the valley were measured against The Great Flood of 1942, a few months after I was born. It forever changed the geography of the valley, slicing hillsides, altering river courses, sweeping away houses, and piling debris and logs high up in the tallest willow trees.

To some extent my father and his two brothers unwittingly contributed to these damaging floods. As young chaps they had each been given an axe, a set of sharp steel wedges, a large crosscut saw, and WERE provided with a rifle and a few provisions. Their 'old man' expected them to clear the bush from the steep ridges down to the river flats. Unpaid, they spent their youth doing this.

The pristine native bush cover held the high rainfall like a sponge. Cleared and denuded of trees, the hillsides eroded and creeks sluiced vast amounts of rushing water down through the valley. The results of this clearing and cutting soon became obvious: destroyed crops, drowned livestock, and farm families faced real danger.

For us children though, floods provided drama and excitement.

The narrow gravel roads were constructed alongside the creeks, so when floods occurred, the roads were often dangerously flooded or impassable because of landslides. Our neighbours had a suspension bridge leading to their house. Whenever there was heavy flooding, they were cut off from the world until the waters abated.

Historic photo of the 1942 Flood. The scene shown here is not in Okoki, but in nearby North Taranaki.

A day off from school was always a thrill for us kids. Afterwards, when the roads were cleared and we were back at school, we swapped flood stories with schoolmates and bragged about who had it worse. Then there were days when we had to leave school early and be driven home before floodwaters made the journey impassable.

Farmers often had to rescue animals from flooded paddocks. I remember my father in his Sou'wester' coat, riding off on his most reliable horse as soon as there was enough daylight to take stock of the situation. With his retinue of barking dogs he moved sheep and cattle to higher ground, and fed out hay to stranded animals. I thought my dad a brave hero on such dangerous occasions. A man against a raging wall of water is indeed a puny and powerless being.

We loved trooping out to marvel at the surging river and smell its pungent flood odour. Dad gave us each a wheat sack for our protection against the weather. With one corner inverted into the other corner, the sack formed a peaked hat and cape.

Dad, restless and housebound by the weather, sometimes nailed tin-lid targets to the old plum tree and had his daughters fire his sleek .22 rifle at the elusive bullseye from the shelter of the back verandah. We loved that, perhaps because those were the only times I can ever remember Dad doing anything playful with us.

Logging was a dangerous and exciting activity. My father cut fence posts out of the tall native timbers. Then, timed with a suitable flood, he and sundry helpers floated the posts down from the head of the gully to where Dad wanted to use them. The challenge was to hoist the posts out and stop them floating further down the valley to other farms. Someone else's posts were fair game if a farmer could pluck them out of the water, as a 'finders keepers' custom prevailed.

There were other challenges too, such as avoiding drowning. Our mother was very tense on those days.

One evening when we were in our teens Dad took me, one of my sisters, and a cousin to our friend's 21st birthday party in the city. Feeling very grown up and special, we returned much later in the evening in heavy rain.

As we drove around a corner down in the valley, we were confronted by a huge slip across the road. Dad drove us back to the nearest neighbours, woke them up and had them phone for our uncle George to come and get us from the other side. In due course he arrived. We had to slog through the rain and mud in our party frocks, clamber up on to the back of Uncle George's truck, then be driven home to tell our triumphant tale.

Here is an extract from an undated letter written by my mother to her sister:

"We were isolated for several days with five slips [landslides] on Okoki Road. The high school children enjoyed it! We played heaps of ping-pong on our new 4-ply pineboard table, which we bought with possum tokens. We had to hunt up DYC yeast and share it around and make bread. Poor Rosie fairly prayed for the flood to keep her from going back to boarding school. But a carload of stock agents gave her a lift back. Got stuck on road between slips. They managed to stagger through deep mucky mud and rang for two cars to come out and bring them to town. So old Rosie lands up with stock agents at Girls High, carrying shoes and with thick mud over her lower half, but a heroine of the first degree."

Country Folk

We country people kept our business very 'close'. Our homes were miles from other neighbours, allowing us the freedom to shout, scream, row, carouse, or anything else families do, in complete privacy.

Mind you, there was the telephone. Ours was a party line servicing a dozen families. My family's number was 63A, that Morse being short-long. We rang these numbers manually and knew a lot about the state of our neighbours by the frequency and flourish of the rings. Repeat ringing gave one much satisfaction.

If we wanted someone urgently, we turned the handle and summoned—long-short-short-long just like the manual exchange. The girls on the switchboard at the Urenui Exchange knew everyone and everything. Short-long-short-long-short-long, they rang.

"That call you put in to the New Plymouth Hospital this morning is coming through now...Hold the line please...how's your wife after her operation?...Putting you through now."

Certain unnamed individuals were, from time to time, thought to be 'listening in'. If that was suspected we learned to convey our messages cryptically. I confess that when our parents were not around, my younger sisters and I sometimes did our own share of soundlessly lifting the receiver and listening in.

They were noble constructions, those telephones. Large

wall-mounted wooden edifices with a handle at one side, a double bell at the top, and housing two generous-sized cylindrical batteries, about 8 inches tall and 3 inches wide. The ringing could be heard from a considerable distance.

The bush telegraph laced with gossip, was the pulsing heart of our district, with its up-to-the-minute information on births, weather, recipes, dramas, accidents, impending visits.

However, there were things we knew *not* to talk about. Our father cautioned us to never disclose how many sheep we ran, how many cows we milked, how many acres we farmed, or how many wool bales we sent off to the Wanganui Wool Sales each year. Dad reckoned that to divulge such information was tantamount to telling how much money we had in the bank. So we learned early to field these questions, which townsfolk invariably quizzed us children about.

We also knew not to disclose family secrets in 'morning talk time' at school, but were quite expert at winkling news of other families through this time-honoured institution.

Few strangers made their way up our isolated no-exit valley.

I recall the Dromorne Linen Man, in his pinstriped suit, amazing us with his luxury-style sheets and tablecloths, which, of course, our mother could never afford to buy.

The Rawleighs Man called regularly and wasn't considered a stranger. In fact, he was a guest at every house he called on. Hot scones and cups of hearty tea were always available. If we didn't have scones on hand, he waited while Mum whipped up a batch. If it was lunchtime, he shared our cold meat and salad. We used and trusted his products: rapid tapioca, wondrous essences, spices, fix-it-all potions, and Ready Relief, pungent enough to keep nasal passages clear with the worst head colds. Yes, we loved the Rawleighs Man.

Sometimes larrikin goat shooters drove up the valley. There was an overabundance of feral goats throughout the district. A carload of young hopefuls, often driving rather recklessly, was easily recognizable by the watchful farming community.

Phones would ring and the unwary shooters were well scrutinized. Dad usually allowed them on our property, with certain conditions, but they needed to ask his permission. If that protocol was ignored he rode up the road on his horse, located the lads and sent them scuttling.

The progress of incoming visiting friends and relatives could be traced from miles down the valley. The phone would ring to say the car had passed Carters' farm. The Wilsons would phone to let us know the car had turned up the wrong road, but was on its way now, in the right direction. Max and Joy would tell us it had just gone past their place. That allowed us fifteen minutes to make the last preparations. Thus we knew, as did all the others on our party line, that our folks were a-coming.

Our narrow gravel road followed the creek, right through to the head of the valley. If we children were walking along it and heard a car approaching a few corners away, we had time to scurry off and hide like pheasant chicks.

My husband recalls his utter amazement when he first experienced this behaviour. A car was heard in the distance, causing us (all teenagers by then) to scramble into the bushes down by the creek, leaving my beau standing there to face the on-coming car, nonplussed beyond words.

The only rationale we could offer was that we didn't want people to know we were on the road, a relic of our historic need for privacy.

I'd like to say the families in our district lived together in pastoral tranquillity and harmony. But this was not invariably so. There were complicated strands of rivalry, jealousy, and distrust between families, with feuds carried from one generation to the next. In spite of these dynamics, we mainly got along with our neighbours, because in such an isolated area we depended on each other for our very existence.

To their great credit, our parents did not discuss adult matters in our hearing. My sisters and I knew little or nothing about the feelings that ran deep and dark between certain folks. Nor were we privy to any skeletons in our own family cupboard.

Only in much later life, I learned from others some of our own family scandals. My parents, loyal and discreet, carried these secrets with them to the grave.

Sundry Pets

From the earliest times our Okoki farm supported a shadowy swathe of cats, ostensibly for the purpose of keeping down the mice and rat population. It was always hard to do an accurate head count, as there were generations of cats, some wild, seldom showing up near the homestead.

Our older cousins told us that when they were young, Dad would offer sixpence to anyone who could catch one of the wild kittens. The three cousins spent hours fruitlessly trying to snare a kitten, which my wily father knew they never could.

There were other cats—well-loved and bestowed with colourful names, that appeared at our back door most mornings. Complicating any cat census was their high mortality rate—with bouts of cat flu and casualties incurred during hunting sorties. Assignations with neighbouring sires and sassy females also diminished the numbers. Our toms sometimes re-appeared after days of absence, sporting tattered ears and sundry wounds from catfights with rivals. At other times they never returned. We usually had about half a dozen cats around the farm at any one time, if you didn't count the old black cat and litters of kittens down by the woolshed that were seldom seen. One can only imagine their toll on the native birds.

Our father had unmentioned means of containing the feline population. Suffice to say, a litter of five kittens might yield only one or perhaps two survivors by the next morning, leaving us children to surmise what might have happened. He referred to these occasions as 'cats' picnic'. Of course he drowned them in the river, as we realised years later. But Dad never spoke about this and I suspect it was a distasteful task for a mild-mannered man who bore no ill will towards any living creature.

Dad had his farm-style de-sexing methodology, referred to as 'gumbooting'. I think he may have put pussy nose first into a gumboot, performing a quickie surgery to prevent an over-supply of tomcats. This too was a taboo subject. My sister reckons our parents were terrified we'd divulge such family secrets during 'morning talks' at school.

We became quite cunning about concealing the silken-soft, sightless little mewlings from the grownups who seemed to be the source of the de-population enigma. Mother cats too, have their own instinct to hide their vulnerable babies, and in spite of diligent searching it was often days before we found where a cat had stowed her newborn family. Tomcats will readily break into the new litter and scoff any male kittens. We once found a kitten's tiny tail, a mute testimony of recent carnage. The neighbours' tomcats always took the blame for this heinous practice. Despite Dad's feline population control methods, he had a great fondness for 'marmalade' cats. Any shade of ginger, in a cat, endeared itself to our father, with these lucky individuals more likely to escape the 'cat's picnic'.

At one time in our cat history we gave all the ginger cats 'M' names: Marmalade (of course), the colour of Mum's robust home-cooked conserve; Muffin, the delicate shade of a fresh-baked muffin; Murgatroyd; Motorbike, who had the sound of a motorbike when purring; and plain-named Michael.

Other cats received equally quaint names. There was Hotrod, whose loud erratic purr reminded us of the neighbour boys' hotrod, and Bobtail, Billy Boy, Valerie, Old Tom, Little Dorrit, Sinbad, Sammy, Wee Willie Winkie, Robbie, and Lavatory Cat.

During the era of the 'M' names we also owned a dear little female fox terrier. She slept in a tea chest on the back verandah. It was rather basic accommodation, with an old sheepskin on the floor of the box. On frosty mornings when we first went outside, a cat would leap out of the box to greet us, then another and another, until about four had arisen for the day.

The long-suffering foxie finally emerged, a little stiff from hosting all her bed companions but definitely warm. She then proceeded to lick all the cats' ears, in the interests of good grooming.

Sometimes a cat (usually female) submitted to being dressed in baby hat and gown, then tucked up in our little wicker dolls' pram to be wheeled along as our pretend baby. This would be the culmination of many attempts to calm the cat while she was dressed and wheeled about. But even the seasoned victim of the pram experience could reach the end of her patience. With a wild look in pussy's eye, she leapt out of the pram and dived into the bushes in all her encumbering glad rags.

Our mother occasionally de-flea'd all available felines. Even the smell of Keatings Flea Powder incited the cats to Extreme Resistance. They escaped at any cost and stayed away until they were sure Mum had ended her campaign. With unsuspecting kittens, she had more success. She generously filled a flour bag with flea powder and tossed the kitten of the moment into the bag, giving it a good shake up. Out came the frenzied kitten, shuddering powder in every direction and desperately racing off into the bushes.

I know our cats performed a valuable anti-vermin service around the homestead. But of far greater significance was the culture of kitty-keeping (or losing) that we grew up with. They taught us to love our pets, to look after them as best we could, and to be touched by their sweetness and softness. This was a great gift to three small girls and their big sister.

Hotrod was a pale biscuit and white cat with some Persian ancestry. He was one of the more famous, making the *Taranaki Daily News* with his frog-catching bender one spring evening.

With much look-what-I've-found caterwauling, Hotrod presented us with a live frog on the front verandah. We delicately eased the terrified frog from Hotrod's fangs and released the hapless creature to its freedom beyond the back verandah. In a reasonably short time, there was more feline fuss, with Hotrod trotting up carrying a second live frog in his mouth. My younger sister gently removed Froggy and again liberated it.

This went on for a total of eleven frogs, one after another. But only Hotrod knew if he was rounding up the same repeatedly, or if it was a bumper evening for frogs! In that same week he brought in a medium sized eel, still wriggling, for our approval and amazement.

Perhaps the most affectionate and loving cat was Bobtail, a longhaired Persian-style tawny brown tabby (named because of a complete absence of any tail). He appeared on the side lawn one day, obviously abandoned, frightened, extremely timid, and resistant to all our attempts at friendship. However, when all was clear of small children, he greedily lapped up a saucer of milk.

For weeks my sisters and I endeavoured to win Bobtail's trust. We put out tempting morsels, which he ate if we were not around. Inch by inch, we coaxed him with delicacies, which he snatched then rushed out of our reach. In a few months we could stroke him, and he eventually allowed us to pick him up. And so we won him over. He had a magnificent bass purr and when carried about, liked to place one paw on each side of our neck, which cats don't usually do.

In the next phase of his life, Bobtail became quite a showpiece. He and my pet brushtail possum Reggie enthralled our visitors with their reluctant stunt. Somehow we coached Bobtail to allow the little possum to ride on his back. Separating the dining area of the kitchen and the side verandah was a stable door. We corralled Bobtail into the dining area and placed Reggie on his back. Poor puss, anxious to be rid of this strange passenger leapt over the closed bottom half of the stable door, with the possum clinging tightly to his long furry coat. Our visitors were open mouthed and implored encores. RIP dear sweet-natured Bobtail and please forgive us for exploiting you for the purposes of showing off to friends and neighbours.

Another stunt that always impressed was when we milked the house cow. Muffin and Mike were our house-cow cats, always on high alert at milking time. They perfected a clever method of glugging down the stream of milk that squirted from the cow, right into the mouths of waiting cats. This was a sure-fire crowd pleaser.

Our most remarkable event took place at the weekends, involving not only cats, but a pet feral goat and Reggie the possum.

We strolled up the gravel road for our weekend walk, Mum and us kids, with Reggie riding the goat, led by one or other of us, and at least two or three cats in tow plus a dog or two. City folks motoring up the road stared in astonishment at our strange retinue. Sometimes they would drive on further and turn around, coming past us again, with eyes agog at this rustic phenomenon.

Farm Dogs

We usually had half a dozen dogs at any one time on the farm too. My father was a great dog-trial man, with many prizes of tarnished silver trophies, cups and trays awarded for yarding and Huntaway events.

Our dogs were born and bred to work. We needed them for mustering the sheep from the steep back country, drafting cattle and generally moving stock from one paddock or gully to another. My sisters and I were never allowed to play with the dogs, even when they were puppies, because Dad said it would make them grow into 'silly mutts' instead of serious working dogs. Dad trained young dogs by teaching them to round up the chooks. When a dog became too eager and started to chase the chooks, or caught them in its mouth, feathers flew in all directions.

I remember one pup had to learn a hard lesson. He couldn't resist the temptation to barge in and chase the hens, and catch a startled chook. This happened a number of times, and eventually he pounced on and killed a slow old black hen. Dad put the dog on a chain, then tied the dead chook around the dog's neck. For the rest of the day, poor doggo was chained up with a mass of feathers under his nose. Every time he tried to drink, the feathers lurched down in front of his mouth, stopping him from drinking. Whenever he lay down, there were the feathers, making it impossible to rest his head on the ground. There was no more chook chasing after that.

Our dogs were vital to our way of farming. The hills were steep, the gullies narrow and the river flats were laced with small dark creeks. The dogs jumped the creeks and swam across them to round up shearing-shy old ewes and their lambs from the bush clad ravines. If a sheep had escaped last year's shearing muster, it would now have a great matted two year-old old fleece looking like a walking mattress with the stuffing falling out. With much barking the dogs flushed these dodgers out of the bush. If we were very lucky a kid goat might get rounded up with them. How we loved the idea of a pet goat! Not so my mother however, with her many memories of pet goats getting into the garden and eating her rose bushes right down to the stems—a goat's idea of ice cream!

Our dogs had many different attributes. Some were excellent 'finding' dogs, picking up and following the scent of a wild pig. Other dogs were able to bail up and hold a pig until Dad and his mates got to the 'barking' dogs and could shoot the pig. One of Dad's best pig dogs met its end when an old tusker fatally gored him as he barked, bravely stopping the would-be escapee from getting away.

The black and tan Huntaway dogs were 'barkers'. The smooth-haired black and white dogs were 'eye' dogs. They were able to control the sheep by eye-balling them. I remember how our mother gave a stern look, when we were being silly in front of visitors. She didn't want to draw attention to us and our foolish ways, so without speaking a word, her eyes told us *If you do that again, there'll be trouble for you, I promise.* An 'eye' dog quietly works the sheep by walking slowly and fixing his/her eyes on it. The sheep know the dog is watching it closely and will usually allow itself and the group, to be rounded up without so much as one yap, from a good 'eye' dog.

Wag was a good barking sort of rouseabout dog, doing all he could to help the mustering if Dad was in command. However, if it was me or one of my sisters trying to motivate him, Wag had a few strategies. First, he acted dumb, looking around making a few desultory barks while feigning ignorance about our commands. *What do you want me to do, Boss?* was the look on his devious doggie face. Or

Can't see any sheep up there, Boss. If the day was hot and Dad wasn't around, Wag's master trick was to bark loudly as he went off to bring back some sheep on a distant ridge. All became quiet, with no sight or sound of the wily dog. After searching, calling and whistling—still no Wag. As we scrambled down to the creek, we often found Wag with only his nose and eyes above the waterline; deliciously cool and wet, perfectly still and altogether deceitful but ready to rouse himself out of the water with an air of aggrieved innocence if we growled at him. However, he was goodness itself when Dad was in charge. *Anything you want Boss, just ask me and the job will be done.*

Another ruse he had was to let himself be deflected by the presence of a possum up a tree. Positioning himself under such a tree and barking incessantly, he tried to dismiss his mustering duties in favour of a bit of blood sport. When our big sister drove the little old Model T truck around the farm, Wag liked to ride on the tray barking extravagantly, all bark and no business.

Wally Frog was my cousin Joan's dog, a longer haired sheep dog, benign in nature and a great farm dog. Wally Frog was a wonderful breeder, giving birth to prodigious litters of beautiful shiny black puppies. One litter produced eighteen of them. We kept one of her progeny, which Joan promptly named Wally Tadpole. The others were sent off to farmers wanting good working dogs, all around the country. They were never disappointed with Wally Frog's offspring.

I suppose dogs, like humans have their different ways, some are Wally Frog types; ever reliable and honest workers. And others of us, both canines and humans, have somewhat flashy and false tendencies.

As for silly old showman Wag, we had a great fondness for him because his treachery was so transparent!

Eels

The creeks of my childhood were narrow, irregular waterways, abounding with eels. To me and my little sisters, eels were anathema—writhing, sinister beings, lurking in the dark, tannin-stained waters, waiting to attack and devour us. One of us could bear testimony to the latter with a tiny scar above her heel where an eel had bitten her. Although shocked and distressed at the time, the surviving victim wore her scar with pride and showed anyone interested the evidence of the frightening attack.

This incident firmly established the unfortunate species as The Enemy—Us versus Them. We were the goodies and they were the baddies. Good needed to overcome evil by whatever means possible. This meant eel eradication, otherwise known as eeling.

Eeling was exciting, dangerous, and more in the nature of a holy war than just a fishing occasion. As we laid our dead and slimy trophies up on the bank, we felt the triumph of The Good who had cleansed our swimming hole of at least some of the Enemy. We crusaders prepared for our eeling massacres by finding and storing rotten eggs. Our chooks roamed over a considerable area so we often came upon a stash of eggs laid in some clever place and abandoned. A smashed rotten egg is vile smelling—one of nature's nastier stenches, but such an egg broken into the water of the creek is an irresistible delight for eels.

The neighbour boys, and sometimes our father,

fashioned gaffing hooks made by bending Number 8 wire into large lethal hooks and attached to a pole.

I am not sure why we went eeling at night. Perhaps Dad considered it a pastime to be indulged in after working hours. Whatever the reason, fishing by torchlight certainly added drama to the whole scenario. The boys from the family down the road a few miles readily participated in the grisly murder of the innocents. My sisters and I were as scared of the big noisy boys as we were of the eels.

When fish hooks were available, we baited them with pieces of freshwater mussels prised from the creek bed and cracked open with a stone. Having a good-sized eel on one's line was truly exciting. They put up a good fight and often eluded us, by twisting and turning and breaking free. When we managed to pull one onto the bank, it had to be put out of its misery with a hearty whack from some sort of cudgel and the hook retrieved.

Nature has provided these creatures with a slimy covering, hence the old saying 'slippery as an eel'. In the raucous process of landing one, cheered on and admonished by all, we became enveloped in slime up to our armpits. It glued sticks, soil, grass and twigs to our hands and clothing. It wasn't easily scrubbed off.

Unlike the Maori, we never ate the spoils of these expeditions. The eels however, weren't wasted. We three children rounded up any available dog-food dish, made a small fire and cooked our eels in water. This was one of our childish delights, poking and priming a fire, watching the eel carcass writhe as the water heated. When it had cooled we fed it to the chooks. Our old black hens picked off every morsel of flesh, leaving an exquisitely cleaned skeleton with its myriad of fine bones. The hens fattened and their feathers shone gloriously on this diet.

Our mother never took part in these proceedings. I wondered if she was repulsed by them. Before she had children she fed the eels in her nearby creek. They became unafraid and Mum grew fond of them. I'm not proud of our slaughtering. I can only plead utter ignorance of the harmless longfin eels* and their enigmatic life cycle. I regret we were never taught to share our creeks with the inhabitants, who doubtless were there eons before we came along with our murderous ways.

~ ~ ~

*The mysterious New Zealand longfin eel with its Maori name of *tuna* is the largest and only eel endemic to New Zealand. They migrate to the Pacific Ocean, probably near Tonga, to breed at the end of their lives. Then the tiny, transparent hatchlings wash to New Zealand shores and make their way to their parents' origins. In their juvenile state they are good climbers and can be found in streams and lakes a long way inland. Many grow to be large and unable to escape from their childhood waterway, spending their lives in confined areas and remote streams. Little is known of their precise life cycle, age or breeding. There are records of females reaching 106 years old and weighing up to 24 kg. They are an important traditional food for Maori. The local Maori once fished eighty eels for a tangi from our favourite swimming hole in the nearby creek.

Pot of Gold

I spent a good deal of my childhood frantically running—bare feet, of course—in all directions searching for that promised, though achingly elusive, pot of gold at the end of the rainbow.

"It's over here!" I hollered over my shoulder to the little sisters who were as determined as I to claim this untold wealth. But somehow it never was 'over here'. I looked again and saw that the end of the rainbow was now up the steep hill behind the house. So upward and onward we puffed and panted, only to discover that the rainbow now ended somewhere behind the house.

Well that was easy, we thought as we tumbled down the hill, tripping each other up in our eagerness to be the first to claim the bullion.

Our bush-clad valley was sheltered from ferocious sea winds and gales. Okoki seemed to gather mists and rain, as a modest woman would cling to her petticoats, and draw the moisture into its damp and darkened self. Rainbows were hence a frequent phenomenon of our wet weather; all providing me with the seemingly endless promise of finding the treasure I so lusted after.

I doubt we had ever actually seen gold in our short lifespans. Our farming life was purely functional with no excesses of jewellery or adornment. And my mother, with her firm Christian faith, decried such fripperies as earrings and bangles.

We read stories of wicked kings, diabolical villains, handsome princes, and beautiful princesses waiting to be rescued, all after the gold had been claimed, of course. I can't recall our parents ever inciting us to believe such tales. They weren't into magic or fairies or Father Christmas. But somehow I fervently wanted to believe that fairy stories and make-believe tales could be true. So there I was running up hill and down dale after the elusive booty at the end of every rainbow.

I don't recall when I gave up running. Perhaps it was like the magic and fairies I'd ceased communing with, where I could no longer cling to my cherished imaginings. They sadly evaporated after a series of disappointments, with fairies failing to materialize and magic proving quite insufficient to resurrect a precious dead kitten.

My mother tried to assure my forlorn self that there were things more precious than gold that enveloped me—sunshine, our beloved bush that clad all the hills I had ever seen, magical views of Mt. Egmont in the distance, flowers in the garden, family, friends, pets.

View of Mt. Egmont

This concept was as equally incomprehensible as other mysteries I could not make sense of: How did eating up my dinner relate to the starving children in faraway India. And where was India? Was it perhaps further away than New Plymouth? If I ate my meal, how would the starving children obtain relief?

At school, when we used a slate and chalk, there was the homily about the children in China not having pencils or paper.

And as for these things reputed to be more precious than gold, to me they were a given. Didn't everyone have flowers in their garden and bush to scramble through by the hour? And if the truth should be known, I didn't actually find the little sisters all that precious.

I vowed that when I grew up I would always wear gold bangles, beads, earrings, large rings upon each finger, necklaces, and signet rings.

In the meantime I made do with curtain rings on my fingers, sometimes as tightly fitting as a tourniquet. I decked my wrists with rubber bands, imagining them to be golden bracelets bestowed upon me by handsome suitors. Sometimes when my mother noticed the tight bands, she hauled them off, cautioning me to never, ever put rubber bands on myself again.

Once, the little sisters and I with our cousins from the next farm were climbing around the hillside dividing the two farms. We stopped to play 'trucks' in an exposed piece of soft and friable volcanic soil, with our sticks, which we used as trucks. There, twinkling in the soil, were tiny glimmers of gold flakes. We had struck it rich! We had discovered gold!

Frantically we dug up handfuls of the mother lode, clenched the soil in our hands and scrambled downhill, and to our cousins' home. We would be famous, yes famous and terribly rich.

Uncle George laughed heartily when he saw our samples. "You've been tricked by Fool's Gold!" he declared. He told us many hopeful souls had been persuaded that this was gold, when it was actually a metal known as pyrite.

How soon and how thoroughly was my gold-bubble pricked as I readjusted to no fame, no wealth, and certainly no undiscovered pots of gold.

Dreaming Through Childhood

From a tender age I was a dreamer. Not that anyone noticed. I wasn't a wafting beauty with grey, faraway eyes or a gentle nature. I was skinny, with stick-straight hair.

I must have suffered from some sort of rhinitis because I was mimicked for wiping my nose with my hand in an upward gesture—the 'hay fever salute'. Because I was an eternal fidget, my mother always suspected I had worms. I was also a tease, annoying the daylights out of my older sister and inciting my younger sisters to occasional caterwauling, fisticuffed, scissor-throwing embroilments. Underneath all this, however, was the dreamer. I believed I was intensely beautiful. In my fantasies I imagined remarkable success at school, with my family and friends paying homage to my good looks and cleverness. I recall my utter shock, when looking in the mirror, and for the first time recognizing how plain I was.

It took a slightly longer time to unravel the fact that I was no star at school, but gradually the realization dawned and I had to come to terms with Me as I was in real life.

The shady, mossy trees of the bush served as background and set for epic childhood fantasies in an enchanted world. Ah, I had another life. I had places under large shady trees, mossy grottoes with their smell of coolness, where spring water trickled. I had an attic—nearly pitch dark, accessible only by climbing up onto the roof of our house, easing my way gingerly across the corrugated iron to a small door. This could be forced open to reveal a deeply mysterious and uninhabitable space, with the open door the only source of light.

A large smooth boulder in the paddock was my trusty steed, as I sat atop of it imagining myself galloping into some faraway distance. It also contained a secret that only I knew about. There was gold, lots of it, underneath the huge rock.

Tienche duck (whose name was a relic of my Scandinavian roots), a homely brown mallard with a limp, knew that I was the beautiful princess, and she, with a drape around her patient if somewhat surprised little head, became the princess's baby. I had generations of kittens, which if they survived the rigours of farm life, slept their nights away with me, snuggled far under the covers.

The bush with its sweet dampness was my enchanted world, wherein dwelt whomever I needed at the time: robbers to be escaped from, maidens to be rescued, or explorers to be heroes.

The Lobby was a quirky little room tacked on to one of our verandahs, with no source of light, other than the open door. It was a place of strange oddments, preserves, shoe-shining gear, sulphur for our treacle-and-sulphur cures and string rolled into knotted balls. All the clutter and clobber of home could be found, with some searching, in the Lobby.

I would stand in there, with the door opened the merest chink, to let in enough light for me to lure the littlest sister in, and then slam the door, enjoying the drama of being implored to rescue her. Sometimes I dared to pull the door shut on myself, enduring the utter darkness for as long as I could stand it, much to the delight of the small sisters. I was in the robber's cave using all my magic to escape into the light and safety.

Dangerous giants and monsters haunted my dream life, too terrible and real to play make-believe with during daylight hours.

One night I had the shocking experience of walking into my bedroom and seeing a giant. I screamed with terror for my parents, who came and found a possum had climbed in my window. Still, I knew with certainty that a real giant had been there.

Another terrifying spectre in my other world was the moon. One of *Whitcombe's Progressive Readers* had an illustrated story of children in bed, frightened by the ghostly shadow of an owl across their window, silhouetted against the moonlight. The illustration of the children—cowering in the dark behind the hideous shape of the owl, with the pale moon lighting their room—left me with a lasting fear and distrust of moonlight and all that lurked out there.

In our pre-electricity house we had no lights to switch on for reassurance, and I knew full well the terrible sweeping, creeping, crackling noises of night.

The severely sawn chestnut trees became platforms of adventure and endless make believe stories for us.

We had several enormous horse chestnut trees that had been sawn down to four or five feet. Branches of re-growth had sprung from below the sawn off area, providing delightful platforms enveloped in leafy, musky-smelling havens.

We played there by the hour, each staking out our own tree, draping string from one to another and hauling up equipment for being mothers, fairies, or neighbours.

In October, when creamy pink spires bloomed, I was a bride, married amidst grand bouquets of chestnut flowers, with their perfume of paradise. One or other of the little sisters would have to oblige as the bridegroom.

Then came the distinct moment, at about twelve years of age, when I could no longer be anything but the real me. I was up a chestnut tree with the little sisters, in full swing, dressing up and pretending—except I could not.

I lamented that whatever it was had gone. It was finished—the make-believe fantasies of childhood were over. I was yet to realize that other dreams and fantasies would carry me through to maturity, adulthood, and beckoning old age.

Today I think about the house I would like to build, the book I would write, of grandchildren, leisure time and contentment, of sudden great wealth. I suspect these thoughts and fantasies may be as ephemeral as my childish world of make-believe.

I reflect on how connected I was to the natural world as a child. Perhaps this could be my 'now' dream: for today's children to have connection with the outdoor spaces of their worlds, wild places that stimulate creative and imaginative play; to do their growing up at a more leisurely pace. There is much magic in every child, so soon lost.

Worlds of Imagination

Rosie had learned to read, and she loved to decipher words on the page. There was, however, precious little in the way of reading material in her household. Although her parents had grown up with a love of the printed page, their old bookshelf contained few books the family owned.

One was awarded to her father as a child for perfect attendance at the bush-school attached to his parents' house. Her mother had a gilt-edged book of Matthew Arnold's poems.

There was the mandatory Sunday reading for all godly maidens: *Fox's Book of Martyrs*. Others, with delicate tissue protecting illustrated pages, intrigued her. Some were too finely printed for a young child to read. Then there was the *Auckland Weekly*, a large, farm-oriented pictorial magazine that gave the all-important predictions of the new season's butterfat, fat lamb, and wool prices. The script on medications, bottles of essence, custard powder packets, and other household products offered further opportunities for Rosie to assuage her hunger for reading.

Rosie's older sister, a veritable bookworm, would in due course bring home books to propel Rosie into the grown-up delights of fiction—classics and modern. But that was in the future.

Until then, Rosie had her own private world of imagination. If she couldn't obtain fairytale books, she could conjure her own world of fairies, with places for them to live, and perhaps be seen. Once she had spied a tiny winged fairy queen. One blink and it had disappeared, of course. The younger sisters helped her provide minute offerings of berries, sugar, and flowers, and were readily impressed with Rosie's first-hand accounts of her intimate acquaintance with these beings.

In another of Rosie's worlds dwelt an array of circus performers. Her family had once been to a circus. Afterwards, the sisters jumped off high branches, rode pussy willow branches as imaginary steeds, cajoled their parents into buying them ball-bearing skipping ropes, and vowed to join the circus as soon as possible. They juggled and clowned. And when their parents weren't looking they balanced on a ladder, precariously straddling their 2-metre-tall concrete water tanks. Then there was the fantastical world of royalty with its retinue of handsome princes, swooning princesses, wicked queens, and despotic kings. Rosie naturally took the plum roles, with the sisters acting as minor players.

On Sundays the sisters converted their secular menagerie into missionaries, preachers, angels, with the odd devil or two. Rosie and the little ones dammed the stream and created lakes to sail across, to rescue the heathen, and spread the word of God.

The farmyard animals tolerated much handling and dressing up. The cats became over-dressed babes in a crude doll's pram, with the occasional kitten leaping for freedom in its encumbering robes. Pet, the old brown house cow, allowed herself to be bonneted and draped as she calmly chewed her cud, keeping her thoughts about this fetish to herself. The bantam hens submitted to being decked out and carried fondly as babies. Tienche duck frequently was swaddled and crooned to, at times listening in mute sympathy to Rosie's crying.

Favourite trees doubled as people and palaces. The soft

volcanic soil served to create highways and hideaways for stowed treasures. Rosie collected river-worn quartz pebbles that comprised the gravel road and stowed them in empty matchboxes, declaring them to be priceless jewels.

These many layered realms of Rosie's imagination fed her soul with colour and drama. They gave her control over kingdoms, bringing luminous beings to life, then just as quickly, extinguishing and banishing them. With little enough to read, Rosie invented and explored worlds far removed from the remote valley of her childhood.

Rosie, in her childish innocence, had worked out Einstein's great truism: 'Logic will get you from A to Z; imagination will get you everywhere'.

Easter

Millenia of fierce flooding, gouging its watery way through the soft mudstone on its path to the Tasman Sea, had probably formed our valley. In this vale, the farming forebears of my family wrestled a livelihood from the land, and we continued the struggle. The rich alluvial soil pumped out growth while the warmth and sun lingered.

Summers were humid, steamy and still. The damp, cool bush hemmed us in from above and the little tannin-stained creek, only a shadow of its pre-millennial self, trilled its way along the valley floor. Tiny river flats and steep eroded hillsides were our farms, our economy—my only known world.

By Easter our short bountiful summers gave way to crisp nights and the first frosts. Mellow days were orchestrated with the languid chirrup of crickets that knew as did we, that winter beckoned.

The sheep had all been shorn and dipped by Easter. Dipping consisted of sending the hapless sheep through a trough of evil anti-lice potion. Plungers submerged the swimming creatures as they frantically strove to reach the end of the trough. De-loused and de-wormed, they were then considered healthy and ready to send to the hills, to gestate and fatten over the winter months. They ultimately provided us with a significant part of the farm income when their lambs were sold to the Freezing Works.

Our gardens spilled out produce. Pumpkin vines inched over tall trees dripping their bright green or silver-grey bounty, held aloft at sometimes gravity-defying heights. Dusty rows of potatoes were dug, yielding sacks of the staff of life. The first sweet corn would be ready to pick, providing us with the unbridled delight and recreation of gnawing cobs anointed with butter and laced with salt and pepper. Our home wafted the sweet winey aroma of windfall apples, spread out on any surface or floor not required for other purposes.

The cool damp nights of Easter brought their annual bonus of mushrooms. Clambering out of bed at daylight became a pleasure for young and old. We scampered around paddocks, our breath steaming in the crisp morning air, filling tin billies, saucepans, enamel basins, aprons and sometimes even beanies. Then back home to breakfast on our pickings. Our mother valiantly fried up pan after pan of field mushrooms as we wolfed down the delicacies. These mushroom feasts were urgent—tiny maggots would soon infest older mushrooms and multiply to the point where the mushies were inedible.

Our first open fires for the season were an Easter ritual. We adored the warmth of our ill-constructed fireplace, huddling around it as Dad poked the large logs and Mother read us stories.

It's strange how memories heal and somehow we will look forward again to the coolness, reach for our eiderdowns and welcome what lies ahead, even if it brings months of raw cold, chilblained feet, leaden skies and a rainfall of eight feet. But for now this is Easter which we cherish, the romantic edge between summer and winter.

Winter Warmth

Winter warmth was hard won in the life of Rosie's childhood. It had to be planned for in the summer months, after the shearing was done, and before the sheep were mustered back into the hard bush country for the winter.

Every member of the family had some role to play in the cutting, and stowing away of wood into the large woodshed. Then, it was a delight for Rosie and the small sisters to clamber into the depths of the shed, atop a ceiling-high mountain of chopped wood. They took extravagant breaths of the sappy freshness of native timber soon to be sacrificially offered in the coal range or on the open fireplace.

Families in the valley thought more of how to cope with the damp cold of winter, than how they would manage the precious resource of native trees.

The family made their annual visit to the old pine tree, with children scampering hither and yon, to pick up cones, always keeping a wary eye out for the occasional weta, terrifying in size and aspect but essentially a harmless insect like a giant cricket.

Wetas, ghosts and giants formed part of Rosie's underworld of imaginings, terrifying and ever lurking in dark or quiet places.

Then there was the pre-winter sewing of pyjamas. Each year Rosie's mother cut out of a large bolt of serviceable striped fabric, every size of trouser and pyjama top freehand. Over the next day or two she stitched the pieces, with magically hidden seams on the treadle sewing machine. Thus was each member of the family kitted out with their winter requisitions.

The garments needed to be twice washed to take out the stiff dressing of the coarse fabric. But such was the excitement of new pyjamas that the children couldn't wait for the weekly boil up of the old copper, choosing instead to go off to bed in the nearly rigid garments.

Pleated tartan skirts on bodices had their tucks unstitched and hems let down to accommodate each girl's growth since last winter. Jumpers were taken out of their wraps and hung on the wire netting fence in a fruitless attempt to remove the pungent camphor smell.

Rosie liked to bury her nose in the woollens and inhale deeply, feeling the icy tingle of camphor up her nose. Mother assured them the smell would stave off every known illness. Gumboots were recirculated according to growing sizes of feet. Each year Rosie silently hoped to have gumboots that didn't leak like the last year's ones.

With the first frosts, came the first open fires for the season.

Gazing into the flames Rosie learned what all lovers of open fires discover. Those flames, ever dancing, exploding with sparks, crackling and hissing, changing the firewood into glowing cities of activity, gave forth the sweet scent of the wood, in its high decibel dying gasps. The searing heat glowed on cheeks, but at the back of the clustered family, the cold claws of winter absorbed any warmth. Shoulders and backs and bottoms needed rotating in order to share the benefits of the fire.

And then to bed, with its zinc metal bottle of hot water, to warm and sometimes blister Rosie's searching feet. The kapok of her mattress enveloped her as she nestled into its lumpy depths. With the feather eiderdown covering all but nose and mouth, Rosie blew steamy breaths into the sharp night air, re-establishing her childish delight in winter warmth.

The Fireplace

Our sitting room fireplace was a large bricked cavity, with a ledge either side and a simple iron grate. Like most open fires, it lost nine-tenths of its heat up the chimney. Inefficient though it was, the fire was our lifeline in the winter.

Each winter evening Dad lit the gas light with a taper of rolled newspaper or matches, taking care not to puncture the delicate mantle which eventually glowed its somewhat meagre light above us. We took turns lighting the fire, which drew us like moths to a flame. We puffed and blew, coaxing the paper and twigs into life, while our parents cautioned us to keep back from the flames.

Evenings for the family were simple and rustic. Our father sat in his appointed chair on the left side and our mother on the right. The sofa was dragged up very close for whoever else was there. That was useful, since barred only by a cotton curtain at the room's entrance, the sofa back cut the draught peeling down the passageway. Any determined draft had easy access to our south-facing sitting room with its one window, two doorways and ten foot ceiling.

There was always a supply of native timber logs for the fire: Totara, Rata and Manuka. We had a large shed, designated for storage and the chopping of wood. From early on, I remember wielding the axe in the hope of demolishing some obstinately knotted chunks. Totara with its explosive sparks was a good fuel for the kitchen cooking range as it enclosed the sparks, but Rata was hottest wood. Each missile from sparking wood had us anxiously searching for the offending spark on the sitting room chairs, the fireplace mat or our clothing. Sundry holes burnt in chairs were evidence of many embers spat out by the warming but spiteful Totara.

Occasionally Dad had an axe head that needed to have the wood burned out to make way for a new handle. This was delicate work. If the heat was too fierce it would destroy the temper of the steel. Gentle embers were adequate to slowly char away the wood.

With a brisk south wind the fire drew best, roaring the large logs into life. On still frosty nights the room was pervaded with the sweet smell of burning wood. A west wind drove alien draughts down the passage, billowing the curtain and causing us to huddle still closer to the fire. But the north wind was the worst, gusting smoke back down the chimney, stinging our eyes, catching in our throats and scattering us back from the hearth.

We had a large cabinet-style wireless fuelled by two sizeable cylindrical batteries. To turn it on, Dad nervously attached sturdy bulldog clamps on to them, crackling our old wireless into life. On special nights we children could stay up and listen to 'Life with Dexter' or 'Dad and Dave'. We were sometimes allowed to listen to the Request Session on Saturday nights. Dad's favourite was 'Silver Threads among the Gold'.

Mum read to us from the Bible, the old classics, Uncle Remus in the vernacular, *Doctor Doolittle*, Banjo Paterson, anything she could find. How hungry we were for stories.

Dad peeled apples from the makeshift winter store, consisting of net wire nailed to four posts. The autumn apples were stored in this hammock arrangement, topped with straw to keep out frosts, with a sheet of corrugated iron weighted down on top—primitive but functional. While Mum read, Dad peeled, offering each slice on the end of his knife. Wordlessly he dispensed apple pieces as we munched and listened. We dried ourselves in front of the fire after our shared bath, while pyjamas were warmed on Dad's knees. We pulled on our crisped night garments, and after goodnight prayers around the fire, it was time for bed.

My parents were all too aware that fire was a terrible enemy. With the nearest fire brigade an hour or more from our house, we needed to be vigilant. One evening while riding home, Dad saw our chimney ablaze. He galloped frantically to the house, and quickly drenching large wheat sacks with water, clambered on to the roof. We made a chain gang and tossed up the dripping sacks which he stuffed over the chimney to smother the flames. The smoke rolled down the chimney, darkening the sitting room. Nowadays this would have been an expensive insurance claim. In those times it was just another chore; a room to be cleaned, a ceiling to be repainted and an occasion for my mother to sew new covers for the sofa and chairs.

There was always the dilemma of what to do with a log not burnt through by bedtime. Sometimes Dad stayed up late until the wood burned down to small embers, safe enough to be left in the grate. A log rolling out of the grate onto the floor was a danger he couldn't countenance. Sometimes water would have to be poured onto a large, partly burnt stump to bring the process to a sudden end. Smoke and steam would pour forth in a spectacular display. Mostly however, Dad accurately judged the size of the wood for the hours of burning we needed. With giant tongs he poked and prodded to re-arrange the embers.

Occasionally the embers were just right for making toast, and no matter how early or late in the evening, supper was on for young and old. We had a long-handled wire fork on which our parents would dexterously prod and balance the bread. Sometimes an errant slice tumbled into the fire, but usually the result was golden toast with that divine flavour and crispness achieved only by embers. With butter melting down over the toast onto our fingers, we were king and queens of the valley, eating the food of royalty.

We had an end-of-winter fireplace ritual. Days before Christmas when the last bitterness of cold weather had passed, the fireplace was cleaned out with tea tree branches tied as a chimney-sweeping brush. We pulled and pushed this contrivance up and down the chimney, Dad up on the roof booming down orders, Mum struggling to keep furniture covered from the diabolical soot, with sundry small children darting about trying to follow Dad's 'do's' and 'don'ts'.

When the whole scene was divested of soot, chimney scrapings and tarry clumps, Stage 2 unfolded. We eager kids collected the blue clay endemic to our area, with the Maori name *papa*. We knew to search for the truest bluest clay we could find, usually a place up the gravel road where a slip had occurred, exposing what we most sought. Then home to mix up a slurry of water and the *papa* in an old cauldron. It was marvellous clay, very plastic and squishy. We painted fence posts, embellished walls of old outbuildings, decorated dog-kennels, and daubed our faces and bodies with it.

A few layers of the *papa* paint transformed the soot-covered bricks of the fireplace, drying it to a delightful bluish white colour. We then gathered pinecones and pine needles to create a display in the grate. No more fire for the next few months. For the next three months, the fireplace would retain its pristine veneer.

They were grand times with school over just before

Christmas for the summer holidays. Excitement of Christmas soon to come and the festive, urgent atmosphere of a 'Need to Prepare All Things for that Day of Days' took over. Let Christmas begin! We swam in the creek, fished for eels, and all helped at haymaking time. After the lambs were shorn, a precious day at the beach left us sunburned and saline. There was an occasional magic night when we took pillows and bedding and slept outside under the poplar trees.

At the beginning of February, the tiny school bus wended its way up the valley, heralding the end of our summer bliss. The blackberry season and sheep dipping were the last activities of our summer. Then the mellow days of April seamlessly ushered in the first nights of frost and once again our family sought warmth and comfort from the old fireplace with its hearty log fires.

Rain on the Roof

Do you hear what I can hear?
It is the rain beating down on the iron roof of my childhood home. Softly at first, then steadily growing in volume—the sound to lull all children to sleep.

There is no insulation between the pressed cardboard ceiling and roof. The downpour builds to a thunderous sound. I, of course, know nothing of the physics of insulation, as I tug the feather eiderdown around my ears and nudge myself a hollow in the old kapok mattress. All I know is that I am safe and warm in the cavernous depths of my musty bed. And outside it is wet and dark.

I wake some hours later, wringing wet. In the darkness I wonder if the rain has poured down onto my bed. My fingers explore the sheets and the eiderdown. The sheets are wet, but the cover is dry. I also know nothing of the physics of a northerly rain system bringing with the downpour humid, tropical air. In other words, I am hot, terribly hot.

Pondering this, I fall asleep, waking at daylight to the familiar sound of rain on the roof. I rub a scribble on the steamed up window, which reveals a sodden lawn and a small river flowing where the path to the toilet should be. My childish heart leaps for joy. Gumboots for the lavatory excursion! I dash to the kitchen door and unscramble a pair of boots, no matter that they might both be for the right foot.

A firm parental hand on my shoulder restrains me from hurtling out into the rain in my pyjamas and ill-fitting boots. I must wear a coat. Ah, but the joy of stomping the sheets of water into spectacular splashes. I return from the toilet expedition with hair wet and pyjamas muddied.

I am eager to explore further. Breakfast must come first, and then, in suitable rainproof clothing, my little sisters and I are off to wade through muddy streamlets, search for duck eggs laid in the creek, and enjoy the rain as only children can.

Calf Judging Day

An older Rosie was absorbed in her gardening, weeding, and watering until she reached a golden privet hedge she and her husband had planted years before. The lemon green leaves, with bees eagerly harvesting the pollen from the tiny florets, stirred a long-forgotten past.

Rosie was a child again in the large and rambling garden and orchard of her youth.

It was November, springtime, and it was a high day in the calendar of her life.

Calf Judging Day was most important and magical day of her whole life, when calves and pet lambs had their day of days. Washed, brushed, transported to school, much was at stake for these prized animals. The winners of the three criteria of excellence: condition, type, and leading, were lauded. And so were their youthful owners.

But Calf Judging Day involved much more than calves and lambs. There were also sand saucers and scones.

Young Rosie could smell the Rhododendron Fragrantissimum, with its riotous heads of creamy pink trumpet blooms wafting an exquisite fragrance of spring sunshine and leafy coolness. With eager hands she pulled off the blooms, straining to bend the substantial branches. Despite the wrenchings each spring, the shrub always seemed to make up enough growth to fill the shady spot beneath a tall pear tree, yielding up its blooms for the next Calf Judging Day. Rosie reached to pluck its blossoms for inclusion in her sand saucer.

Industrious bees hummed their work-song and like the child, bumblebees searched for easy blossoms to reach. She longed to do what one of the older boys at school had demonstrated once or twice: clasp a bumblebee with bare hands. That had given him hero status on each occasion. However, she wasn't willing to risk a sting with no one but herself to appreciate such an achievement.

The sand saucer competition was always a highly competitive event among schoolchildren who combined sand, flowers, leaves, seeds, and other found objects to create an artistic and (they hoped) winning tableau.

Rosie searched for forget-me-nots to decorate her miniature garden. Like tiny galaxies, the blooms twinkled from the shaded and shy areas behind the house. With a horseshoe nail and infinite care, she would press each flower into the damp saucer of sand, making a symmetrical pattern. Such a piece seemed the epitome of created beauty. Nothing in her experience looked so perfect as the concentric rows of royal crimson Sweet William flowers, contrasting with the intricately placed rows of forget-me-nots, set off by laurel leaves tucked around the entire edge of the saucer.

The laurel tree grew over by the woolshed, its dark strong leaves used by her mother and grandmother before her to bestow vanilla flavour to blancmange. Rosie breathed the perfume of the creamy flowered spires, and amid the bees she grasped for leaves within reach. With its blossoms and bees, it now created a sort of ecstasy of the senses. At other times of the year the laurel tree smelled musty and seemed dreary.

Returning from the woolshed, Rosie searched for moss for her miniature garden. Handfuls of the bright green moss were stowed into a large treacle tin. She scraped lichen from apple trees, plucked tiny ferns starting and ending their brief life in a shady crack on the pathway to the front gate. Her mother's small hand mirror was rummaged from the depths of a large, floppy and faded false-leather handbag to create the pool, which nestled in the moss. Twigs were found and sorted for rustic fence posts. Rosie would be allowed to take a tin tray from the kitchen to display her garden.

Back at the house her mother stoked the coal range so Rosie and her sisters could bake their little batches of scones, hoping for them to be judged the most evenly raised, delicately browned, and uniform.

And then, finally, Calf Judging Day arrived.

At the school, plates of three scones, identified only by a number, were displayed on long tables in the classroom, to be judged for excellence, along with chocolate cakes and pikelets.

When the judges finished their work, the children surged into the transformed classroom, now a wondrous cornucopia of baked goods, flowers, tiny gardens and sand saucers. It was a joyous burst of colours, textures, with smells of ovens, and springtime. Then gasps as the children searched for the winning entries. Red cards stood beside first-place handwriting, floral work, and cooking. Blue cards signified second place, gold cards for third place. Eagerly Rosie searched for the red card and was devastated to see that it rested on someone else's miniature garden. She lacked the dexterity to make a miniature garden to equal the creation in her mind's eye. Her gardens always competed poorly with the superb constructions of older pupils.

Rosie could not know these childhood memories would serve as beacons to draw from deeply for the rest of her life. In places and times far removed, she would once again feel the smooth perfection of a mud-lined thrush's nest and recall the sweet damp of water-trickling in mossy places.

In the arid climate of her adult home, she would remember a bumblebee fumbling its greedy way into a flower and the waft of the Fragrantissimum on a gentle spring morning.

Chamber Secrets

The door closed behind them, leaving the little sisters in darkness, allowing only a thin chink of light under the crudely fitting bedroom door. That slice of evening light greatly comforted the two small girls, symbolising the life that lay beyond it—the warmth of the farm kitchen, the low sounds of mother and father talking, and the benevolence of the old wood-fired stove with its hot-water cylinder emitting the contented trill of near-boiling water.

Within the dark room was the shared warmth and security of each girl positioned 'top and tail' in the weary bed, with its wirewove sagging and kapok mattress unable to do any more than soften the sag. The children rolled the tin bed-warming bottle in every direction. The woollen jumper that swathed it jiggled loose, exposing the heat of the naked metal and causing each girl in turn to exclaim and wriggle away from the burning canister.

It was Friday night, the night Mother sometimes accorded the little ones privileges not allowed on school nights. The last time they had been allowed to top and tail they had awoken the next morning to a wet bed and the reek of warm stale urine, each sister accusing the other of the crime.

There was the excitement of proximity. The girls sang every song they knew, then making up songs and challenging each other to compose yet another, singing and giggling and comparing ditties.

The mother came in, gentling and shushing them with her callused and chapped hands. The children's faces seemed soft and petal-like to her touch, whereas the mother's hands on the little girls' faces caused them to exclaim at their roughness.

The door closed and this time there was no light from the kitchen and no more quiet conversation. The darkness was invasive and sinister to the little girls. They were glad of the presence of one another and soon fell asleep, with the bed-warming bottle kicked to the far edge of the bed.

The chamber pot was usually, if not reliably, stored under the bed at night.

Sometime in the night five-year-old Rosie woke her older sister. "Sis! Are you awake?"

A semi-conscious mutter escaped from the sleep-sodden sister.

"I need to do a wee, sis," Rosie whispered.

With some effort her sister opened an eye. "The chamber is under the bed," she muttered.

Rosie scrambled out from the covers, landing on the floor, along with the metal bed-warming bottle. She squealed in fright at the unexpected clunk. Her sister had receded into the depths of sleep and heard nothing.

Rosie felt her way along the bed and with her fingers explored timidly under the sag of the wire wove. No chamber pot there. Edging along and fumbling with the desperation of a refugee clinging to the safety of an island lest she fall off the edge into unfathomable depths of the ocean, Rosie groped in the return direction for the chamber.

"Oh sis, I can't find the chamber!"

Another grunt from her sister as she rolled over.

"What'll I do?" Rosie's cry claimed no response. She fumbled the length of the bed, with one hand holding the safety of the coarse grey overhanging blanket and the other hand exploring the cosmos below the bed for the pot.

Eventually, bladder relieved, Rosie crawled her way back to the warmth and nestled below the covers.

First out of bed next morning, Rosie's sister loudly lamented that her sock was wet. Indeed, both socks were sodden. She called indignantly to her mother—"There's water on the floor and my socks are dripping!"

Mother and sister came into Rosie's focus.

As Rosie opened her eyes wider and beheld their faces, inquiring and accusing, she put her head under the covers and wailed loudly, "I couldn't find the chamber!"

Potato Stamp Redemption

Although Rosie had learned from earliest infancy about Heaven and the narrow path of obedience and virtue that led to it, she had allowed her nine-year-old self to be tempted right off that path. Her sinful act preyed heavily on her mind, depriving her of any joy the rest of her world seemed to revel in. All around there was fun, school noise, and laughter.

Rosie, in contrast, was an island of guilt, gloom and fear. To miss out on Heaven would be unconscionable, forever separated from her beloved mother and even the pestiferous smaller sisters.

Rosie had a heavy dark doubt about where her father was heading, for he was not yet a Believer. Perhaps she could be with him, she thought, brightening a little. But then she reflected that mother and children prayed every day that her father would come to love and obey God and give up smoking. So maybe it meant only Rosie would be severed from Heaven and family.

In a maddening torment she kicked the schoolyard dust with her Roman sandals, causing gravel and sticks to lodge under her toes.

The shed where Rosie wrestled with a potato stamp–and thoughts of Heaven, obedience, and virtue.

All the children in the shelter shed at school had been making 'potato cuts' and creating deliciously bright repeating patterns. The tempera paints used consisted of a few basic shades and were dull of pigment but to Rosie's colour-hungry soul, there was amazing and rapidly achieved beauty at the end of the potato. Each child took a turn to whittle a cut potato face into a stamp with a shared, square-ended, blunt knife.

After an interminable wait, Rosie's turn with the knife would enable her to at last create a wondrous potato stamp. Eagerly she cut into her potato, soon finding that corners were a problem. Try as she might, Rosie couldn't get a relief sculpture that resembled anything she had in mind. Other children were jostling her for the precious knife and quite soon, she was without knife, observing her misshapen potato cut. "Looks like a cow's tit," scoffed one of the boys.

As she dipped her potato into the paste-impregnated paints and stamped it across the page, there was more hilarity. Even when the teacher intercepted, the boys silently mouthed "Cow's tit, cow's tit." Shamed and disappointed beyond words, Rosie wiped off her potato and threw it at the loudest scoffer. Her love for potato cuts had turned to loathing, all the more so when she saw Betty Mack's flower designs wending their elegant way across the page.

Rosie's potato stamps were far from elegant.

At playtime when all eyes were upon Betty Mack's sleeping doll, and every girl was lined up to have a moment of holding the wondrous thing, Rosie spied Betty's potato, lying unattended on the long seat inside the shelter shed. With no thought for her eternal consequences, she scooped up the potato and tucked it into her bloomer leg. Now she would be able to make exotic flower patterns with every paint colour.

Hungrily, Rosie imagined paintings on the wall; patterns on her journal cover and praise from all that beheld them. Only then did it occur to her that she could never display her beautiful designs, not to anyone because, of course, all would recognise Betty Mack's potato cut.

Suddenly she felt only heaviness, with the coveted acquisition failing to bring her the joy everyone was having. The potato now seemed to burn with an unbearable and satanic heat where it touched her skin. By this time there was a general search in every dark cranny of the shelter shed, with Betty Mack in tears, comforted by the doll holders.

Rosie knew what must be done and done quickly. Ducking her head under the long seat, she fumbled the potato from her bloomers, smelled it to ensure there was no telltale bloomer pong and called out triumphantly, "Here it is Betty!"

"Good on you Rosie," praised the all-wise and kindly teacher, "I thought you might be the one to find it."

Rosie glowed with pride and felt immeasurably relieved. Far better to go to Heaven with most of her family than harbour the potato stamp. It was very pretty, though....

What Rosie Saw

The 'new' Okoki school that replaced our two-room school after it burned down in the 1950s. The Okoki school has been long since shuttered and is now used for other purposes.

Rosie had witnessed something she knew to be wrong, terribly wrong. At nine years of age, she could barely articulate the terribleness of what she had seen and smelled. There were others, though, who were older and bolder than her, and they told the teacher.

The headmaster of the two-teacher school was relieving at the school whilst their beloved Mr Harris was away from school with illness.

Mr Milford, a placid pipe-smoking man, short in stature but long in sense, dealt with the situation admirably. He questioned each one of the twenty or so students away from the eyes and ears of others. "Where did it happen?" he asked Rosie.

"Up in the plot," she stammered.

The so-called plot was a steep rise at the end of the ample flat playground. It had been planted out at some earlier time with gum trees, which had now matured to a lofty height. It was in the plot that arguments arose and were settled, pecking orders were established, huts were made and unmade. Once or twice there had been reports of spitting, swearing, and even kissing.

Away from the scrutiny of their teachers, it was an opportunity for some of the older boys to establish their own Lord of the Flies community. Dan Johnson had ruled supreme, until he was almost killed as pillion rider on his brother's motorbike. Dan spent the rest of his primary school days at home in plaster from neck to ankles, waiting for all his fractures to heal and his voice to break. After that, there was more freedom but definitely less law, as this awful day attested to.

Afternoon session was hushed as each child was called to the staff room for questioning. Heads down, but ears alert to any new developments, children tackled their schoolwork as never before. At length the three miscreants were called for and left the room together. The air bristled with the electricity of expectation. Each child worked tensely, in abject silence, waiting to hear the telltale sound of the strap being administered. But no such noise emitted from the next room. For the rest of the afternoon the boys were absent from class, with Mr Milford popping in at intervals to keep the work ethic honed to unprecedented perfection.

At last the bell rang to end the school day.

One by one, the three boys emerged from the staff room, as pale as death, one vomiting in the school corridor. Amazement and fear grew, as slowly the boys admitted to their fate. Rosie felt frightened but oh-so-righteous as she viewed the misery of the terrible three. Riding home on the bus, the usual noise was reduced to gossipy whispers and furtive glances at the boys.

Out of the bus, Rosie raced the remaining mile home, on winged feet. Being older, she headed off her sisters pushed through the doorway, holding the two younger girls back as she fairly exploded to her mother. "Mum, Mum! Guess what! Three boys were smoking up in the plot today and Mr Milford made them all take turns to smoke his pipe and Brian was sick up in the corridor. They all nearly died. Oh it was awful!"

Winners & Losers

There was an outbreak of marbles at the little school in the valley. This was a yearly occurrence, precipitated by the crisp days of late autumn, after the summer cricket season had subsided, and before the winter basketball season took hold. Rosie had enjoyed cricket. Using some of the more robust primer children, there were just enough students in the school to cobble up a couple of teams. There were frequent opportunities to sit out on the bank, waiting for the most luminous batspeople to be bowled out. Much more fun than doing sums or spelling.

Now, with the first jangle of marbles in someone's home-sewn marble bag, Rosie was seduced by the time-honoured sport. She couldn't decide which she liked better—the tortoise shell swirls on opaque milky white, or the glass marbles with wondrous air bubbles.

The visiting blacksmith, whilst shoeing the horses, heard Rosie whining for marbles and imploring her mother to sew a marble bag. "Got something for ya Rosie," he announced on his arrival the next morning. He extracted a small packet of marbles from the pocket of his leather apron. "If you turn the handle of the forge for me I'll pay you with these."

Anticipating her reward, Rosie cranked up the forge with joyous vigour, making galaxies of sparks hiss and swirl as the nest of coals glowed red hot and hotter. After his supply of coals had diminished in record time, the blacksmith pleaded for a slower and more sustained winding of the handle.

Her cup of joy was full and overflowing when she poured her newly earned marbles into her hand and discovered a large Tom Bowler. The huge marble reflected dancing light from its mysterious internal bubbles, giving it the awe and importance of a royal orb. She gasped and fingered it reverentially until she was reminded to "Say thank you to Mr North." Her mother sewed a marble bag from a cut-down shirt sleeve. Although it was hardly as nice as Jillian Cole's pink gingham one, or Judy's maroon velvet bag, Rosie appreciated that it would do the job.

Monday morning could hardly come soon enough for Rosie to jangle her marble bag on her wrist and display that kingly trophy, her Tom Bowler.

At school, games of marbles were played according to the strict classification of Funsies or Keeps. The younger and less shrewd players generally called for Funsies, which meant each player retained their own marbles, regardless of who won or lost. However, Funsies did not attract the adventurous or risk takers, or allow the opportunity to increase one's stash. Sometimes it was hard to find anyone to play with, so safe and tame was this game.

It was Keeps that drew players like moths to a candle or flies to a spider web. Daring and dangerous, this was where high stakes were lost or gained.

Rosie well knew the skill and guile of the big boys. She was reluctant to let them even touch her precious booty. But after a few "Wows" from several of the boys, she let them hold the Tom Bowler momentarily, never letting her eyes stray from it in enemy territory. Even Doug Jones was nice to her and offered her a game. Funsies, of course. Which he lost. Quite a few games later, he was still the loser. Rosie swelled with pride each time she trounced him. She was turning into a better player than she could have believed.

When he cautiously suggested a game of Keeps, Rosie agreed, confident in her new found prowess. Again she aced him, and this time he must surrender his marble. Triumph was hers. Three more marbles found their way into her homely marble bag. Doug now called for Tom Bowlers. As she fished out her precious marble, Rosie breathed on it for good luck before the game began. There were near misses for both of them, when suddenly Doug's Tom Bowler rolled on its fateful collision course, hitting Rosie's marble.

"Mine!" he claimed as he snatched the marble. Rosie was aghast. Fortune had come to her and now it had gone.

"Look it's alright," comforted her predatory partner. "Try and win it back from me."

They agreed if Rosie won, he would return the Tom Bowler. Rosie's confidence was displaced with desperation. Focussing as she had never before, she flicked her marble, but could not reach the enemy. Then *wham*, a sickening sound of marble against marble, and Doug Jones had won back the first of his decoys. Then ... the second and ... the third.

Rosie realised she'd have no marbles left if this went on. She kicked the damp sand, and with a look of venom cast at him, she walked off, minus the love of her life. Then turning around she intoned the lyric that she and her sisters and cousins had always cursed the Jones boys with:

> Douglas Jones a bag of bones
> And a tummy full of fat
> When he dies the flies will cry
> What d'ya think of that!

Whereupon Doug Jones merely poked out his tongue and held Rosie's Tom Bowler up at her, with a taunting grin.

Blue Satin Dress

Rosie Carter's time had come. It started with the arrival of a new teacher, Miss Carter. Miss Carter was young, smiling, and carried a waft of marvellous perfume as she tossed her curls from her face.

Rosie, sharing the same surname, was imbued with instantaneous importance and status at school. The older girls let her use the big toilet hole designated for girls in Standard four, five, and six only. Betty Mack shared her sleeping doll and Jill Cottonwood gave Rosie one of her sandwiches with hundreds and thousands sprinkled on, their wondrous colours mixing in the warm butter.

Of course the boys didn't count. What would boys know or care about being important? In fact the boys seemed determined to ignore such a quality and applied their writhing, wriggling, punching, elbow-jolting energy to taking importance down. This revelation was definitely not for the boys.

That first morning when Miss Carter introduced herself, the children, stunned to silence in awe and expectation— had answered self-consciously as she called the roll and looked into each face, making her own private appraisal. When she reached Rosie's name, she smiled warmly and said, "Rosie, I see that not only do we share the same name, we have the same birthday month."

Rosie's body stiffened with unspeakable pride and ecstasy. Next month she would be 10. Her course of action was clear: She would ask Miss Carter to her house for her birthday tea. Miss Carter would come with a birthday present wrapped and ribboned' imploring Rosie her to unwrap it and wear it immediately. Inside, there would be a blue satin party dress, with a huge bow and lots of lace and ribbons and buttons and ric-rac braid.

Even the boys would be impressed. "Miss Carter gave it to me!" she would say as she walked past them, in her stunning pale blue satin. The big girls would dote on her, bestowing eternal favours. And the boys would keep a respectful silence, desisting from their abominable teasing and name-calling. Miss Carter would choose Rosie to tidy her table each afternoon. Miss Carter would say, "No, I'm sorry, you can't sit there. That seat is for Rosie." Rosie and Miss Carter would sit together and have lunch, while others watched wistfully. Miss Carter would make the boys write a hundred lines saying *I must not tease Rosie.*

Somewhere between roll call at 9 o'clock and morning playtime at 11 o'clock, Rosie's world of what was, and the enticing spectre of what might be, spun itself like a spider's web into a delicately draped reality. Rosie whispered her information to her best friends of the day. They in turn whispered it to the lesser best friends, until all the girls had been apprised of the situation. No boys were let into the confidentialities. They kicked the dirt and each other, indignant that the girls were up to something.

The story grew with its repeating until the entire female population of sixteen knew it: Miss Carter was Rosie's cousin and she would be coming to Rosie's birthday tea next month, with a beautiful dress for Rosie: pale blue satin, with a big bow at the back and lace and buttons and ric-rac braid. But it had to be kept a secret because Miss Carter didn't want everyone to know, especially the boys.

Mavis Kent, the oldest of the girls, allowed Rosie to ring the bell to end playtime. Basking in new privileges and pleasures, Rosie allowed the puzzled boys to push past her unhindered as they elbowed each other back inside the classroom.

Somewhere between the end of playtime and the beginning of lunchtime, another reality began to dismantle Rosie's web of fantasy. Mavis Kent and the older girls had time to ponder Rosie's claims, finding them to be dubious. Lunchtime led to Rosie having to defend such questions as "How do you know she is giving you a blue satin dress?" and "How come Miss Carter didn't tell us you two are cousins?"

Rosie thought quickly. "That's because of the boys, silly. She doesn't want any of them to know."

The girls understood this well, as they watched the boys for once on the outside of things, disconsolately mooching about with nary a girl to goad or push.

"How come Miss Carter said she is coming to your birthday, anyway?"

"Of course she's coming. My mother said that only my cousins can come."

"Are you going to *her* birthday?"

"Course yes," snapped Rosie. "She specially wants me to come. And my Mother says I can give her a present too."

"What is it?"

"Mum says I'm not allowed to tell. Not until it's her birthday."

"When is her birthday?" Mavis Kent asked with tactical triumph. "I bet you don't know."

"I do so," retorted Rosie.

"When?"

Her mind racing, Rosie gasped a desperate gulp and declared "It's on February the 30th!" Mavis Kent snorted so long and so loudly that Miss Carter strolled by. "What's making you laugh, Mavis?"

Rosie looked at the ground and wished desperately that

Miss Carter would ask no more questions. The teacher walked away, then stopped. Turning back, she looked into Rosie's face. "You and I will have to share our birthday party this year, Rosie."

The bell rang, the boys jostled the girls to be first in the school door and yet another fragile reality was evolving for Rosie. Like a spider web, re-forming in the coolness of the night, it lay somewhere between what was and what one wished it might be.

On the Bus

Enveloped in a coat of sorts, rather too short in the sleeves but nevertheless offering an adequate buffer between her and the winter cold, Rosie stomped around on the road trying to keep warm, waiting for her sisters. Both younger than she, they had not yet caught up.

"Hurry up!" Rosie bellowed into the frost. "I can hear the bus!" That wasn't exactly true, but it served to panic her sisters into a final desperate dash to the small wooden bridge.

This was the designated extent of the bus run. From there on, the gravel road narrowed and was not considered safe for the bus, leaving a mile to be raced down from their house in the mornings and dawdled up in the afternoons.

The gravel road from our house to the school bus stop.

Rosie gazed at her bare feet, toes pink and swollen with the cold, promising chilblains when she warmed up. Her stomach rumbled. She fossicked in her school satchel, pulled out her two egg sandwiches and ate them. Next came the jam sandwiches, with the jam not yet sunk into the bread and therefore still palatable. She would save the windfall apple for lunch.

Hearing the bus wending its way up the road always gave Rosie a feeling of excitement and anticipation. And gratitude. When she had started school the only transport was the big car, owned and driven by Mrs Smith, and sometimes by Mr Smith.

Small children like Rosie had to sit in the back seat on the knees of the big kids. Three of the smallest were sandwiched in the front seat beside the driver. Rosie found either option highly uncomfortable. The big boys on the back seat unceremoniously bounced the small kids seated on knees, and as the car lunged around corners, every last child would be deposited into in a squirming heap.

A Bedford school bus, the iconic workhorse of rural New Zealand school transport. Painting by Wallace Trickett.

In the front seat Rosie detested being nearest to the driver, as she found herself invariably obstructing the tall gear leaver, which had to be shifted frequently.

A few years later the Smiths' car was finally replaced by the twelve-seater Bedford bus.

The bus, resplendent in Education Board colours of cream and maroon, offered the luxury of a seat for each child. When the bus arrived the three girls surged through the door to secure the best seats. Being first on the bus bestowed considerable bargaining power. Rosie could use her favours to great advantage during the day. Allowing Carol to sit up the back with her could win her a piece of chocolate cake. If it was June Collins, the booty might be a dainty white bread sandwich, sprinkled with 'hundreds and thousands' and the crusts cut off. Or perhaps being allowed to hold Betty Mack's baby doll.

There were risks, though. Grant Setters could well bunt Rosie unceremoniously from her seat, taking it for himself. She hated Grant. He had white frizzy hair, something so alien to her world of dark straight-haired people. He'd moved from the city and Rosie surmised that only townies had pale hair like his.

Today he was content to merely taunt her. "My dad reckons Reggie should be shot!" Yesterday she had brought her pet possum Reggie to school for the day. Rosie had been the epicentre of interest and importance that day. Only the best of yesterday's friends had been invited to hold Reggie. When he became startled and scampered up the headmaster, sitting on that worthy head, it was Rosie who was able to dislodge the little brushtail possum, without injury to Mr Harris's rather vulnerable scalp.

But that was yesterday and today the wretched Setters boy was declaring Reggie a pest. Rosie swung her satchel at her tormentor's head.

Now the Taits were filing into the bus, all four of them smelling of fried bacon and urine. Grant Setters turned his attention to them: "Pink, pink, your knickers stink!" An exchange of punches left the Tait children settling unwelcomed into seats as the small bus rumbled on.

As the bus warmed, Rosie's chilblains began to appear. She scratched frantically, firing them up to a brilliant pink and unbearable itch. Swapping her windfall apple for a pale green conversation lolly, Rosie read its message: 'You are my true love,' before stowing it into her jacket, making sure the delicacy was not in the holey pocket.

It felt like a very good day for Rosie. The conversation lolly might even buy her a longed-for lesson with Valda Hodges at playtime, when Valda might teach her a ballet step. If that didn't happen, she could pass the sweet, with all its written significance, to the school hero, Barney Lamb. She could probably wheedle a jam sandwich from one or both of her little sisters. And perhaps, just perhaps, she might find her missing shoes and socks today.

"If Grant Setters has thrown them up into the rimu tree, I'll breathe on his lunch every day for a whole year," she vowed.

After School Adventures

Coming home from school was an experience to be anticipated and savoured. Pupils on Rosie's road had to wait at the school until the 12-seater bus delivered other pupils on lesser roads first.

Mr Harris, the headmaster, with music spilling from his fingertips, allowed the children waiting for the Piko Road bus to push the chairs and tables to one side, then opening up the ancient piano he would play folk dance tunes. How the young dancers loved their routines, singing lustily "the side two couples will do-si-do, parlez vous, the end two couples will do also, parlez vous."

All too soon it was bus time with dancing ending abruptly as jostling children vied for best seats. The children then sang every song they knew, coming home on the bus:

Blue smoke goes drifting by
Forever and ever, my heart will be true
Irene good night
You are my sunshine
Zing zing zoom, my little heart goes boom
Between two trees
Sweet Vio-lets

This was a time when even crusts of sandwiches, rejected at noon, now seemed appealing to the ravenous. The bus reeked of stale sweat, punctuated with pickle and jam, and perhaps a well-travelled banana.

The gentle, good-natured bus driver was accommodating in every way. Bill Tindal was a bachelor boy, unused to bringing unruly children to order. Predictably, he was open to cheerful manipulation.

On one particular afternoon tiny speckled pheasant chicks came into view, dashing off the gravel road into the long grass.

Piko Road in Okoki.

A chorus of "Bill! Bill! Can we please get out and catch them?" persuaded the mild-mannered Bill to stop whilst the children spilled out of the bus, diving into the long grass, after the pheasant chicks. Predictably the chicks, more cunning than the children, eluded capture.

Sometimes at the end of winter, native clematis with its

pristine white flowers dangled down from trees near the road. Once again, the obliging Bill found himself waiting as children scrambled up the bank and clawed down the vines of the exquisite blooms. It mattered not one jot that the clematis flowers wilted within hours of being put into a vase of water.

Then there was the time at the end of the bus run the six remaining children spied a cluster of feral goats with two very young kids. Throwing schoolbags to one side the children scampered up the hillside after the tiny goats. "Wait for me!" was the wail of the smallest sister. But no one on this tantalising mission could do any waiting. On and on they scrambled, up one hillside and down the other, with the goats just beyond their reach.

Rosie would show her cousins how she could indeed chase and catch a goat. The day was warm and the goats were sure footed. Young Trevor Johnson tagged along, slightly ahead of the smallest sister, urging the others, closing in on one of the bleating kids near enough to 'spit in his eye'.

Rosie rounded on him and bawled out, "If it hadn't been for you, yelling out like that, Trevor Johnson, we could have nearly caught that little black one. Just shut up and keep chasing!"

Over another hill, now nearing the bushline, some hasty decisions had to be made.

Rosie's cousin, Dennis, by virtue of being three months older than Rosie, was the undisputed elder statesman. "You all wait here quietly and I'll creep up into the bush and chase the little goats down, then you have to rush and grab them."

Simple! Or so it seemed, until at last the goats reached the safety of dense bush and disappeared, never to be seen again.

Dense bush provided refuge for wild goats in Okoki.

As Dennis returned to the group of flustered and sweating would-be hunters, a familiar voice was heard calling in the far distance: "Den-nis! Ca-rol! Ron-ald!"

And then another familiar summons: "Ro-sie! Gra-cie! Bet-ty!"

"It's our mothers!" someone yelled—everyone knew what that meant.

Rosie's mother and aunt were justifiably cross. Very cross. These benign beings tolerated the children paddling in the creek or running home around the hill tracks, but this was unacceptable. It hadn't dawned on the children that their mothers would be worried they had left the bus more than two hours ago.

Back at home Rosie's mother smacked her with a ruler, which made Rosie giggle at the ineffectual punishment. "You're the oldest and you should know a lot better than to wander off like that."

More whacks with the ruler, and more giggles from Rosie, ended what had been a fruitless but altogether memorable goat hunt.

Nights on the Front Verandah

As soon as the long New Zealand winter showed signs of abating, there was the ritual moving of beds onto the front verandah.

The end of the verandah, where the beds were placed, had a return of about one bed length. Two beds would be arranged there, leaving a narrow access between them.

The third bed and its occupant had full benefit, or otherwise, of fresh air, wind, frost, and rain.

Before bed the girls bathed in the nearby stream.

Once in bed on one of those nights, and excited beyond sleep, three small girls giggled and chattered their way to exhaustion at last. Sometimes on one of the hot nights of driving, tropical rain, bodies and beds had to make a dramatic retreat. There was a special significance to Friday nights. In the summer the family bathed in the creek, with plenty of soap and jollity, dodging the odd eel. The girls would then fly straight to bed.

To their delight, the evening meal was served to them in bed, stories read by a mother so exhausted she oft times read herself to sleep. But with a nudge and a wake-up joggle or two she struggled on until the words again became slurred with weariness.

Many a good book was shared in this way. *Tales of Uncle Remus*, read in the vernacular, and *Dr. Doolittle*, with his magnificent push-me-pull-you, became an integral part of the children's heritage of fantasy.

Then, as the late dusk merged the bush into silhouettes, stars were born in the newly darkened sky, and Ruru Owls cried their plaintive *more pork*. With kiwis screeching their demands to the moon in the soft darkness, the chatter gradually diminished, each child dropping off to sleep.

For the mother, this evening was her own precious spare time. It was many years before the girls realized that Friday nights had been engineered by their mother for her greater benefit!

If the rain held off, the lambs were weaned and the ewes were shorn before Christmas. Nights on the verandah then became a special delight. Tired children were lulled to sleep by the myriad calls of the lambs, bleating and blaring on every note of a sheep's octave, their calls overlapping, achieving a cacophony of bovine noises. Children and animals gradually became still and quiet after a day of high activity in and around the shearing shed.

In the school holidays their older sister returned home, claiming the least lumpy bed as her right and reading far into the night, with a candle, fending off the odd bug or wiping a moth from its waxy doom. There was an eleven year age difference between youngest and oldest. The four-year-old was still crayoning her primitive drawings on the pressed metal wall, whilst snuggling in behind her big sister who would be reading Steinbeck.

Warmer nights heralded the migration of the girls onto the verandah to sleep, lulled by the sounds of the bush and the farm animals.

Tinges of autumn, the evening air sweet with wood smoke, and the first early frosts, were signals for the girls to migrate back to their indoor bedrooms. A sharply cold wet winter followed, leaving the children waiting for the cycle of seasons to bring again those warm nights on the front verandah.

An Okoki Christmas

Christmas punctuated our farming year with an exclamation mark! The school year ended with our big sister home for the holidays, the four of us girls threw ourselves into the family's Christmas preparation countdown activities.

There was mustering and shearing of ewes, weaning of lambs, and sometimes we even managed to get our hay paddocks mowed and baled before Christmas, depending on the fickle subtropical summer weather. Then there were our annual rituals, such as painting the old open fireplace with slurry of blue papa clay to extinguish any sign of winter's soot. A decoration of pine branches and cones in the fire grate looked very splendid and suitable as a Christmas decoration.

When we were old enough to assert ourselves, we decreed to our busy parents that we must have a tree. A few non-native pines dotted paddocks far from our house. Three small girls and the big sister set off with an ancient and barely functional pruning saw. Hours later we returned home, triumphantly shouldering what was to be our Christmas tree.

Young *pinus radiata* trees have an open, sprawling look about them with a few scraggly branches and tips usually forming a cluster of newly hatched bristles–hardly a festive look. Dad gave us a spare kerosene tin and plonked our tree in it, shoring it up with large stones. We were more than delighted as sweet turpentine wafts of pine fragrance filled the house. We cut crepe paper streamers, used the foil paper from Dad's cigarette box and improvised with every sort of bauble we could create, to festoon our tree.

The business of making puddings was a major undertaking some weeks before Christmas. The copper needed to be filled with water and heated to a merry boil. With her bare hands, Mum mixed lashings of suet, sugar, dried fruit, marvellous aromatic Rawleigh's essences of rum, vanilla, almond and lemon, many eggs and much flour.

We vied for positions of mixing, breaking the eggs, measuring ingredients, sifting flour, and of course licking the spoon or scraping the bowl. We collected threepences from Dad's pockets, boiled them for a few minutes and tucked them into what would be our own family's pudding.

Calico flour bags made the best pudding cloths. Multiple chubby round puds were tied and immersed in the scalding copper. Keeping the fire beneath it burning vigorously was all-important, as the water must not be allowed to go off the boil. After what seemed many hours, each pud had to be fished out of the cauldron, with the 'copper stick' (a well-worn sturdy length of some branch).

Mum and our big sis hung each pudding out on Dad's S-hooks at the back verandah: one for our grandparents, one for great Aunt May, another for a neighbour, one for us and another for New Year's Day, and a spare for someone else. As the days passed and the puddings dried, they looked woebegone, wrinkled, and even mildewed, but we well knew that on their resurrection, they would emerge fully flavoured, plump, and steaming.

The Christmas cake was another fully integrated activity. Sometimes Mum used the dry ginger ale recipe, with or without a tin of crushed pineapple. Other times, she followed a recipe that incorporated prepared custard.

The icing was a major pleasure—regular white icing covering almond icing. The exotic almond paste, only ever bought at Christmas, was such a temptation to us cake makers that we dug into the semi-malleable block and scoffed it greedily when Mum wasn't looking. Those recipes are long lost, but the finger-licking sweetness of the mix remains in my taste buds.

Mum liked to coach us in singing carols. The soft grey and white illustrations in the red Christmas carol book transported us to some other world with turbaned wise men, a babe in a straw manger, strangely shaped eastern-style domed buildings—and always that massive star. Mum pedalled the ancient pump organ, urging us to sing along. By Christmas Day we had grown rather tired of singing carols but Mum was determined, as was Dad, who couldn't carry a musical note in his body. So carol singing was a mandatory interlude on December 25—preferably before any guests arrived.

Our animals were also smartened up for Christmas. The chook house needed raking clean and new hay in nest boxes. The unwilling cats required a dousing of flea powder. The dog kennels were straightened out and the dogs scored an extra large lump of goat meat. The gardens were tidied and lawns mowed.

On Christmas Eve, Mum's lisle stockings were at a premium as we each placed one at the end of our beds before we retired. When we awoke they would be stuffed with irregular shaped lumps.

Dad recalled his childhood in the bush when a Christmas treat of great significance was an orange in the bottom of the stocking, and nuts. So Dad relived childhood memories when each year he stowed the self-same duo down in the foot of each stocking.

Unshelled mixed nuts were very secure against small children. We bashed and hammered away with whatever we could find. Suddenly with one last blow struck, the kernel would be revealed, flattened into the ground and inedible.

Our Christmas Day always began early. Very early. Shortly after 4 a.m I was up and fumbling for my bulging Christmas stocking in the pre-dawn light (no electricity, of course). Then waking up my sisters, we rushed upon our still sleeping parents, with our rustling and unwrapping of gifts and squeals of delight.

Over the years some of the gifts we found included jigsaw puzzles, colouring books, Lakeland coloured pencils (guaranteed that the lead would break whenever we tried to sharpen them), boxes of water paints, bloomers, hair ribbons, combs, brushes, clips, pyjamas, socks, singlets, hankies, an atlas, puzzle books, four-inch high pink plastic Kewpie dolls, and mouth organs. One year we were given a cricket set. Another year, tennis rackets.

Presents opened, it was then on to preparing our Christmas dinner. There was the stove to be lit, a pud to boil its way back to life, and the ritual digging of the very first new potatoes from the garden. These had to be washed under the strict supervision of Dad, who wanted his precious newborns to be gently scrubbed and rubbed to remove the delicate skin without molesting the body of the spud. The shelling of myriad new peas seemed an unending task. Making the mint sauce was a job I liked.

First we gathered a fistful of the best mint shoots from wherever they had spread in the garden, and avoided picking any within range of the farm dogs weeing on them. The leaves needed to be chopped finely, ready to be steeped in the sugar, vinegar and boiling water, eventually emitting a pungent aroma. Making stuffing for the roast lamb and dressing the meat were tasks we adored. All of these chores formed our Christmas rituals year in and year out.

Now I would like to invite you to our Christmas dinner. Welcome Ken! Come in Michael, you too Nerida. Hello Margaret and Bill, so glad you could come!

Dad is sitting at the head of our old wooden table. The more sprightly of the guests can sit around the back on the old bench worn smooth by many sitters. If we put the slimmer ones on the bench we can fit four. So that's Dad at one end, two more at the other end, four on the bench and four on the other side. We'll need an extra stool and the chair from the sitting room. Don't worry about the kids. They can all squeeze in at the table on the side verandah.

Mum is bringing over the pot of minted peas and the roasted veggies. As Dad carves the lamb the minted new potatoes appear. Such mouth-watering smells. Mum passes around the stack of mismatched plates. Dad places the sliced meat on each plate, taking good care to serve up the best bits for the women. Then Mum takes each plate and serves the veggies. Dad goes on carving for the kids until there is a jolly plateful to be passed over the stable door to ready takers on the side verandah.

Help yourself to gravy and mint sauce. Could you please pass the salt and pepper? Mum says grace and all may start on this banquet of entirely homegrown food.

The veggies are then passed over the stable door to the side verandah for the 'littlies,' but Mum comes out to supervise the gravy and mint sauce, which will need to be apportioned out if any on the kitchen side of the stable door want second helpings.

Second helpings make it difficult to accommodate the pud and cake that finishes the meal. Mum bears the steaming rejuvenated beauty to the table. Dad again does the honours, carving up wedges, each with solid guarantees of containing a coin, for all the wrigglers on the side verandah. Vanilla-flavoured whipped cream tops each serving of the pud.

Over the stable door go the bowls. Dessert plates of every shape, size, and design have been called forth for the occasion. "Not too much for me, thanks," you murmur, regretting that second slice of lamb with another pouring of gravy.

On the side verandah there are exclamations of surprise and pleasure as coins are discovered in the puds. Then all is quiet as the kids speed outdoors to further adventures. That leaves the satiated adults undisturbed to sit at leisure with cups of tea while Mum whisks away the plates and the leftovers.

There are oohs and aahs as Mum brings out the Christmas cake. It is cooked to perfection and iced by eager hands, creating a somewhat whimsical and rustic finish.

We exchange many a yarn in this setting. With the charisma of a real raconteur Vic tells amazing tales of pighunts in our bush. Dad always has an account of some practical joke he has played on an unsuspecting neighbour, leaving us all laughing until tears come.

Now it is milking time and some of you must depart to attend to your own chores.

It was a pleasure to have you. Where are the children? As you call their names and cooee up into the bushline, first one then another and then the whole bunch of them emerge, rattling down the hills to the waiting cars. Merry Christmas to you all!

Mum's Christmas Cake

Note: I once squeezed Mum's Christmas cake recipe from her. She was never very specific and found it hard to write precise directions. I admit I've never baked it, probably because it was short on instructions, though I gluttonously enjoyed her cakes for many years at Christmastime.

10 eggs, separated
1 ½ lbs flour
1 lb sugar
1 lb butter
½ tsp nutmeg
2 tsp spice (mixed)
1 tsp cinnamon
½ tsp cloves
½ c golden syrup
1 lb citrus peel
1 pkt raisins
3 lbs sultanas
Add egg whites last
Combine. Cook 5 hours. "A cooler oven brings out the flavour (so they say)."

Backstage on Christmas Day

In my earlier story I perhaps conveyed a memory of Christmas that sounded too good to be true.

Blessed to have memories of love, family, acceptance, friendships, comforting rituals, and parents who didn't burden their children with the harsh scenarios of the adult world, I now have some understanding of what such an occasion as Christmas must have cost my mother. And possibly my father.

So come with me to the backstage of our Christmas celebration...

On Christmas Eve, with the myriad farm and house commitments completed, parcels wrapped, and stockings filled, Mum and Dad have gone to bed late, exhausted. All too soon they're awakened for that day of days. Their work begins.

Mum's first duty is to light the coal range, which is truly the working hub of the house. She blows paper and kindling chips into life. Soon the whistling kettle makes ready for Mum to brew Dad his morning cup of tea—one sugar, no milk.

While the children are preoccupied with dressing and trying out surprise gifts, Mum slips away to dig a hole for the contents of the family's bucket toilet, years before we had a flush toilet. For some reason that is always seen to be women's work.

Then back to supervising us girls feeding the dogs and

the chooks. We wash and have our hair plaited. While we gobble a hasty breakfast, the large cauldron on the stove is boiling and ready for the Christmas pudding. Mum has clambered up on an ancient chair to release the pudding from its hook at the back verandah.

Dad takes a couple of us out to help gather his prized potatoes, the first of the season. He forks the ground with utmost sensitivity, while we are instructed to rummage around for Dad's booty like truffle pigs, carefully placing the creamy white potatoes in a basket, ready for our Christmas meal.

Dad also supervises preparing the lamb roast. Actually, he does the instructing and Mum does the work. There must be the right amount of salt rubbed in, plus pepper. Then there is the stuffing: breadcrumbs, fresh herbs, egg, onion finely chopped, all of which must be added precisely to Dad's directions (as if Mum doesn't know about these matters).

Mum stokes the coal range—feeding its hungry gut with aromatic native timber pieces. She opens the oven and sniffs the heat. Still not hot enough. More wood. She opens the oven and sniffs again. Oops! Too hot. Put the damper in and wait a few minutes. Another sniff into the oven and Mum is satisfied. In goes the lamb, with Dad's blessing and Mum's hard labour. We carry in more armloads of wood to be offered up as the morning goes by.

Phone calls are made to friends, relatives, and neighbours, wishing them the compliments of the season. Dad is very faithful about communicating with kith and kin.

Mum sniffs and bastes the roast at intervals, while trying to tidy the kitchen, keep dishes done, preparing the pumpkin and stoking the fire. Tough pumpkin skin makes cutting the pieces for roasting a hazardous business, so only Mum wields the cleaver, tussling with the smooth rounded pumpkin which will deflect the knife into your hand if you are not fully alert.

Shelling the new peas involves anyone dodging other chores, such as setting the table, rounding up chairs, ironing the huge damask tablecloth, or finding tumblers for each guest. We shucked and shelled endlessly, until a very large long-handled saucepan was three-quarters full of the greenest, sweetest peas imaginable.

Before we owned a kerosene fridge, the process of making whipped cream took good planning and watchfulness. The cream mustn't be too fresh or it won't whip. Storing it for a day or two without it going sour is tricky, especially in humid weather. And keeping the cream in our outdoor safe has its challenges. We wrap the bowl in a damp tea towel and keep it in darkness to avoid the light tainting it. Today it must be beaten with the eggbeater, in preparation as its star accompaniment to the Christmas pudding. I turn the handle until my arms ache; it seems to take forever before it thickens. One wind too many and the cream would curdle. To avoid such a calamity Mum oversees the process with vigilance.

Somebody remembers that the house cow hasn't been milked! Pet, our sweet natured red-brown cow, allows us to milk her any place, any time. However, she has a definite understanding; if she has wandered down the gravel road towards the house and nobody shows up to milk her, she may take herself off for the day.

So I am chosen to go and find her. I don't want to be away from this hive of excitement and expectation. I wander up the road yelling "Come on, Pet!" but she isn't falling for that. She tucks herself away in some quiet bank above the creek, out of sight. Unless one walks right past her, the cunning old bovine can't be found.

Eagerly I scamper home declaring that Pet is 'lost'. Not so, corrects Big Sister, who seizes a bucket and strides up the road, winkles Pet from her hiding spot, urges her unceremoniously down the road, and soon has a bucket of the best.

Mum unearths the huge damask tablecloth that does its annual duty before it is taken to the steam laundry in New Plymouth to waits for the next Christmas. It looks resplendent on the old wooden table. The next challenge is to round up cutlery and dinner plates. Every odd knife, fork and spoon is rallied to active service. We remember Dad doesn't like a fork with 'lugs' on it, (the little flourishes that ornament some forks, just above the prongs); he also he has his favourite broad bladed knife.

We count the number of places, the number of guests, the available plates and cutlery and hope it will all tally somehow. Then for the table on the side verandah, the kids can have the small bread and butter knives, the second-rate forks and odd spoons.

Gravy making is another of Dad's specialties, again mainly consisting of instructing Mum on the finer details of the process as she pours the fat from the roasting dish after the lamb has been cooked to mellow perfection. "Don't pour all the fat off," he cautions.

Mum, not a fan of mutton fat, tries to keep as little as possible, but Dad's watchfulness prevents that notion. The juices from the roast are mixed with just enough flour and water to make the gravy thick and rich. The large old roasting pan is scraped and stirred, with many more instructions from Dad, who seems to think our mother couldn't make this without his explicit advice. Mum patiently continues stirring and thickening until Dad is satisfied.

Big Sister finally drags Mum off to be beautified. The phone rings. One of the neighbours a few miles down the valley has just seen the green Chevrolet of some of our visitors.

With whoops of excitement the little sisters and I rush down to the front gate and wait with desperate anticipation. We scarper around, jumping up and down with all the energy of small children. At last we hear a vehicle in the distance. We run down the road to greet the car and run beside it as it pulls in to our gate. We are ecstatic with delight.

There are hugs and greetings and "My how you've grown!" exclamations as we escort the visitors up the path to the house. We wheel and circle like a pack of excited husky dogs. Let Christmas begin!

Memories in a Blackberry Jam Jar

Blackberry picking in Okoki was the communal business of farm wives and children. I can remember my father only once being prevailed on to help. The cleared river flats readily gave way to blackberry invasions as the brambles thrived near water. These bushes, unnatural as they were to New Zealand, provided a reliable bounty of luscious blackberries. But we had to work hard for our reward.

To a small child these were grand days of fun and freedom. We swam in our bloomers in the tannin-dyed creeks with their dark-tea colour.

There were picnic lunches followed by hours of romping in the fringes of the bush as our mothers picked.

Nibbling at the purple-black nutty tawa berries with their turpentine taste, fallen thickly on the ground, we peered at the native pigeons in the branches high above us gorging on the same ripe fruit.

As we grew older and were more useful with picking, each of us was given a treacle tin with a wire handle. That's when the fun ended and the real task of picking began. Oh, the devilish sandflies that bit us without fear or favour. Many a small billy of berries was spilled as we swatted a maddening marauder.

Then there were the thorns, ready to painfully rip bare arms and legs. We usually wore gumboots but where rubber ended, sandflies and thorns began. After a day of blackberrying, digging out prickles was an evening's sport. How eager I was to needle out others' prickles and how reluctant to trust anyone to operate on mine!

Our mothers toiled away by the hour tipping their filled billies of the wine-sweet berries into kerosene tins, taking care to include enough red unripe ones to provide the pectin for jam making, avoiding the ones with maggots in them, and leaving the dried-out overripe berries for the birds. Those were our instructions as we toiled under a warm sun. Entwined with the aroma of blackberries was the warm sweet smell of grassy meadows, punctuated with the low hum of bees gathering pollen from the pungent pennyroyal. The crickets chirruping their autumnal prelude knew better than we that summer was coming to its inevitable end.

The days of making jam are also sharply etched in my memory. Every small jar we could scavenge was cleaned and sterilised in the wood oven, ready to be filled. Great pans of berries boiled up over a furnace of heat. Oh, the sweet perfumed elixir that was hot blackberry jam! Flushed with heat, our mother stoked more wood into the ever-hungry firebox and stirred the pans of bubbling berries.

White mounds of weighed-out sugar were poured in at just the right time, and then a sample would be spooned out on to a saucer. If the small dollop of jam formed a skin, it was ready to bottle. We funnelled the molten purple flow into hot jars and there it was—our blackberry jam, that fusion of sun and summer and bountiful rain, uniquely flavoured and wondrous in colour.

In later years when European wasps became ubiquitous, the aroma of hot blackberry jam attracted them by the hundreds. With adroitness born of much practice, and some small amount of cruelty, we would press a wasp against the windowsill and squish it with our bare fingers. But there were myriads more to take its place. We trapped them by luring them into bottles of sugary water. We tracked them to their nests and burned them out, but made little impact on the huge population. For all their nuisance and painful multiple stings, we seemed to accept the wasps' inevitability. They became as much a part of our summer as the jam making.

There were blackberry and apple pies, sponges and sometimes just the fruit, cooked up and still warm, with thick scalded cream on top. How our mother must have toiled to achieve all this.

My memories, however, are of whole days of busyness, filled with purpose and occupation and fun for each of us children. We scrubbed out jars, licked wooden spoons, and dampened the cellophane top for each jar, securing it with a rubber band. We wrote out little labels. Then came the satisfaction of seeing dozens of jars, with their magnificent contents, cellophane seals dried taut and concave, all stowed away into our dark outside storage room known simply as 'the lobby'.

There was also the joy of sharing. We would take blackberry jam to our grandparents and various friends and relatives in town, who always cherished the little jars we proudly presented.

Nowadays when I buy a jar of Cottees blackberry jam in the supermarket, I take one sniff and for a fraction of a second the memories flash back, vivid and poignant. They take me back to a time when my world was that of a child, safe and surrounded by those I loved, with the sweet smell of blackberries steaming away on that old wood stove.

Food Fit for Children, & Pigs

My mother was attuned to serving any food she thought might be considered vaguely nutritious or healthy. She was decades ahead of her time. When she started making cottage cheese, her mother-in-law declared it to be 'pig food'.

Dad fed our pigs skim milk, which in warm weather naturally soured overnight, producing the curds and whey the pigs relished and that Little Miss Muffet was famous for. Mum believed curds and whey was perfectly healthy fare for humans, too.

Our pots, pans and utensils were likewise basic and utilitarian. Our meals were plentiful but very basic, and mum made most use of those ingredients that were local, plentiful, and inexpensive...or free. Some of the dishes she came up with were delicious. Others were a bit more challenging, particularly to youthful palates. Here are a few that I still remember:

Cooked Watercress

Mother made lavish (and economical) use of watercress, which grew wild in our streams. Watercress eaten in its raw form in a salad is delicious. When cooked, however, watercress takes on another life. It becomes a vivid green with a sharply unpleasant taste. Traditionally Maori have cooked watercress with meat, such as pork or mutton. The fat mulls the sharp flavour, making it a bit more palatable. Our mother, alas, thought it a healthy stand-alone food, not to be adulterated with animal fat. In spite of her threats and bribes, I seldom could bring myself to eat this dish without serious gagging.

Bread and milk

As children we grew up hearing that prisoners were fed a diet of 'bread and water'. Somehow my childish mind converted this to be 'bread and milk'. It puzzled me that the wicked people in prison should enjoy what was my favourite breakfast treat. It was a hand-me-down from my father's childhood, when the austerity diet of his times would have highlighted bread and milk for breakfast as a treat. Here's how you make it.

Cut cubes of white bread and place in a saucepan of milk. This must come to the boil, to reveal its full flavour and slightly slimy texture. There must be plenty of the scalding milk for the bread cubes to absorb. Serve in a bowl and pour honey or sprinkle brown sugar lavishly over the top. A drizzle of cream on top finishes this to perfection. (Lucky prisoners!)

Jerusalem Artichokes

My mother used to make thick, fully flavoured soup with Jerusalem artichokes when they were in season. (Jerusalem artichokes aren't true artichokes, but are a sort or tuber, or root vegetable.) I liked everything about these artichokes, except the eating of them. To my childish palate, the flavour was strong and obnoxious.

The plants sport golden flowers on long stems, rather similar to a sunflower plant. My younger sisters and I willingly burrowed around the roots, searching like truffle pigs for the tubers, with their distinctive wart-like growths.

When we scrubbed them under a cold water tap their skins would shuck off easily; revealing these naked, creamy tubers, waiting to be cooked thereby revealing their full vileness.

Yeast Drinks

In her bread making heyday, mum famously made small, firm, wholemeal buns. They were nutty, nutritious, and popular with one and all. In school lunches, they provided me with good bargaining power for lunch swapping. From the bread making came the idea for making yeast drinks. Mum would mix warm water, yeast, and a little sugar (brown, of course). This mixture would stand in a tall jug, beside the coal range, overnight.

The next morning she would stir the fluffy 'head' that had developed and would pour us each a tumbler of this slightly fermented, intoxicating beverage—with as it happens, no discernible nutritional benefit whatsoever. We drank it readily and Mum's heart must have warmed at the thought of the yeast drink 'doing us good'.

Junket

Although our meals were simple, there was always pudding

(dessert) after our main evening meal. Junket and stewed rhubarb was my favourite. To make junket, my mother used Renco, the trade name for rennet. (Rennet is, of course, an animal enzyme used to start the process of making cheese.) She would add a small amount of Renco to a bowl of lukewarm milk, which would magically transform into a velvet-soft curd. Nutmeg sprinkled on the top made this a complete delight.

When we had junket at our grandmother's it usually contained slivers of ice, since Nan had the luxury of a refrigerator. My sisters and I considered this slightly icy delicacy food of the gods.

The Dromorne Linen Man

Townsfolk who visited us in Okoki Valley imagined our lives to be blissfully pastoral. They sat at our table eating banquet sized meals of home-killed lamb, with vegetables freshly picked and committed to the pot. Hearty puddings with lashings of the thickest scalded cream sealed their notion of our life in the country as unending bliss.

A stroll up our little gravel road, peering into the dark depths of our tannin-stained creek with huge dragonflies hovering at its surface, along with the chortle of song thrush and the sweet smell of damp coolness confirmed our habitat as a virtual paradise.

For us who dwelt in Utopia, however, the reality was somewhat different. Our family all worked hard. There were chores for the children; unending toil for my mother, and my father's farm work occupied all the hours of daylight. Dad never considered the option of coming in to a meal until darkness had curtailed his activities.

Then there was the weather. The valley in winter was damp and cold, and black frosts were common. Endless drenching days of fierce, sub-tropical rain contributed 96 inches of annual rainfall. Our benign little creek became a milk-coffee monster, raging its way down the valley, scouring out roads, hillsides, and cutting us off from the world.

We were all involved in pitting our lives against the elements: moving stock, clearing the road of logs, digging slips over the road, driving a sick neighbour to the doctor, and feeding out hay to stranded animals. Even with oilskins and gumboots, we were soaked to the bones, only to be revived at home in a hot bath, with clothes dried out for tomorrow in front of the old wood stove.

Summers were short and humid. There was an orchard of fruit to be picked. Pickles, jams, and preserves had to be set up for the winter. The kitchen garden needed to be planted, weeded endlessly, and harvested.

Shearing and haymaking drove us all to heroic efforts, as we strived to have the lambs shorn by Christmas, the hay baled before the fickle weather broke, and the main shearing finished in time for the first Wanganui wool sale of the season.

My parents had no leisure time and holidays were unheard of. For the farming families in the valley there were few occasions of reprieve from work.

The annual school picnic at the beach each summer was an agony to me. Our family always had to leave at the glorious height of afternoon fun to go home and milk cows. Ping pong at the hall on winter Saturday nights, an occasional Beetles Night (an innocuous dice game accompanied by a monumental supper), and the monthly Anglican church service, dry as a tack, were our few moments of escape from chores.

Into this setting came the Dromorne Linen Man. Year after year he made his way up the valley, calling at each home to display his exotic and wondrous wares. The Dromorne Linen Man was notable for his appearance, which contrasted sharply with the Rawleighs Man, an honest-to-goodness sort of bloke wearing an open neck shirt.

He was immaculate. Children in the Valley had no contact or experience with immaculate men.

Our fathers and neighbours had hands hardened and

calloused with toil. Their clothes were basic and functional: baggy slacks, a coarse tweed jacket, sleeveless V-neck pullover, hand-knitted in the ubiquitous post-war grey wool—a comfortable uniform, worn to occasions such as dog-trials, sale day at the stock yards, school concerts, and town days. Everyday farm clothes were dungarees, held on hips often with strong twine, or more usually, braces, and a black bush singlet.

Our men had the familiar smell of strong soap, pipe smoke, sheep, cows, and horses. But this man had an unfamiliar, metallic whiff of cologne that raised my suspicion. Country children hold high stock in smells. At an early age, I could smell rain, fear in a horse, and the right heat for our wood fed oven to cook scones. As an animal is alerted by an unfamiliar waft, I sensed difference and danger in its strange allure.

We were all riveted, mouths agape, by the Dromorne Linen Man's shocking departure from right and proper maleness. His thin, sandy-straight hair was parted perfectly in the middle, lying obediently flat on each side.

A deportment of serious importance wafted about this man who insisted on a cleared, clean table to display his wares. He wore a tie, pinstripe trousers and a black jacket. His fingernails fascinated me—so unlike my dad's ragged and ridged nails—hands not to be trusted with their alien smoothness, I thought. Nor did he speak in the ways of us country people. His words were clipped and tight, hemmed in by smileless thin lips.

As he unreamed bedsheets glorious with the sheen of linen, richly hemmed and smelling of newness, he asked us not to touch them. Reverentially we recoiled, deeming the sheets to be hallowed because of their untouchableness. A half-century later, I can understand his distaste for small children, usually grubby, darting around his pristine wares.

We were amazed and enraptured as he displayed his

fine linen.

Our beds were made up with coarse twill sheets, obtained from Farmers store, purchased for their cheapness and durability. Never did we dream of sleeping between such luxury as those shown by the Dromorne Linen Man.

The towels he unfolded were huge beyond belief and thick-piled, pale in colour, exuding a subliminal message of a life free of mud, rain, and gumboots. Our own towels, also from Farmers, were in serviceable colours such as brown, caramel, and strident pink to 'not show the dirt', with pile as rigid as any back-scratching loofah.

He laid out richly embroidered pillowslips and facecloths with embossed satin hems. I imagined a life of bliss and ease, with me in the midst of these trappings. Emerging from a bath full of hot water (our baths were always brief, shared and with small amounts of water), I would wrap this robe of pastel towelling about me and then sink between the magnificent sheets.

We gasped at the tablecloths, ironed flat and creased perfectly to unfold and cover our tired old wooden table with a mantle of superb elegance. Gone was the oilcloth cover smelling rankly, its printed design long lost by regular wiping. I imagined myself dining in undreamed elegance.

Demonstration over, I marvelled at the Dromorne Linen Man's ritual of folding everything perfectly with those pale, smooth hands meticulously packing and stowing away the linen.

He solemnly accepted an afternoon tea, country style, then bid my mother a laconic good-bye and was gone, without a smile, or, needless to say, a sale.

And I was left with my own set of fantasies about the Blissful Life.

My Paternal Grandmother

Crabbit and crochet, with choker pearls
Henna dyed hair, fine-rimmed glasses,
Semi quaver of hand and structured curls
Frame a withering stare, as she passes.

Joyful children all beware
Our grandmother wastes no smile on us
Let no children linger there
She shows no hint of fun or fuss.

Destiny heaped her share of pain
Where once she had hope and golden beaches
She toiled so long for little gain
Now she has learned what a harsh life teaches

Where once there was warmth, it has frozen to cold,
Dreams have withered as the woman grew old.

Doors & Scents

Click! The door closed behind her. In all of her young life Rosie had not been used to doors that shut.

The lavatory up the back yard steps overlooking the valley had a door that could never be operated. Father was poor in carpentry skills. And why would one shut out the morning sun and the mist below it? Bedroom doors likewise were left open, always. And although the bathroom had a door, it didn't shut. A curtain and a discreet cough warded one off from the outside world of kitchen and the large handsawn table.

The front door could not be pulled quite shut for some historic reason. Its majestic key in the lock was an elegant decoration and a sometime plaything. All these deficiencies constituted Rosie's unshackled freedom.

And now at her grandparents' house she was placed in bed and with a click of the door all Rosie's freedom evaporated. Darkness and a shut door brought panic to her five-year-old self. Clasping her teddy tightly she lay, listening to the foreign creaks and crackles of the night. A double bed for a small child is a vast area, cold in the corners, hard of mattress, with alien spaces unknown in Rosie's history of beds.

She remembered the electric light. Groping around in the darkness, high above her head, she located the cord and gave it a desperate tug. On off, on off, she delighted in this novelty. Nowhere in Rosie's home could there be light at the pull of a cord. On/off/on/off/on again gave her an idea. Up she leapt and began bouncing on the bed. Up and up she jumped, landing gloriously on the mattress below her. She bounced higher and higher, landing with delicious tumbles on the bed until she eventually wearied.

She noticed two large scent bottles on the austere, dark oak dressing table. Easing out the glass stopper of first one then the other, Rosie discovered the lure of sweet smelling perfume. She tipped up each bottle in turn, pouring into her hand the elixir of love and romance. She dabbed herself all over until the smells merged into something sublime and indescribable.

More jumps on the bed, more cord pulling, on/off/on/off and then finally sleep came.

The next morning as Grandmother surveyed the wildly disturbed bedding and sniffed the telltale perfume, she decided that the little alcove off her bedroom, with its small stretcher bed, would be a far better place for Rosie to sleep.

Funeral

One morning before dawn, Rosie's mother woke the children. Nan was dead.

As Rosie struggled to understand what this meant, she heard her father weeping. That was the most disturbing and unnatural of all. There was no cue for her to comfort him, so she crept into his bed and lay close into his back, hoping desperately that his tears would soon finish.

Her parents decided that the three girls should attend the funeral. This was a shattering of propriety. Children were considered much too immature and ill-formed to cope with the gravity of such an occasion. On the day of the funeral, relatives from far and wide arrived: grand aunts and uncles, with suits and fob watches, black coats and fur foxes with pointy noses intact, the old ladies with brightly rouged cheeks, scarlet lips and the waft of wintergreen and camphor. Grandfather was hedged about with the black clad camphorous relatives. Rosie recognized this as the smell of oldness. Various elders appraised her, noting how much she'd grown, which Rosie always hated.

Rosie was allowed to see Nan at the viewing. Cautiously approaching the coffin, she looked at her grandmother lying peacefully. The lines of suffering and harsh frontier life had been gentled. To eleven year-old Rosie, she seemed to be sleeping and entirely rouseable.

"Wake up Nan," the little girls whispered urgently, waiting for a flicker of the eyes.

Any slight movement would reassure Rosie that Nan would be alive again. This must surely happen. With increased vigilance she waited and watched, but grandmother did not waken. Rosie cautiously touched the expressionless face. It was not a caress or a touch of affection, for there had been little affection bestowed by Nan, or for that matter by Rosie. Rather, it was a curious reconnaissance, to ascertain what it might feel like ... to touch death. And death felt unfathomably cold, and wrong.

Rosie had seen death before, in newborn lambs too weak to suckle, succumbing to the chill of early spring frosts. The last two kittens she had chosen, from litters doomed to be disposed of, had reached only fluffy adolescence. With coughing, and streaming eyes, their mewing became weaker until the beloved kittens finally lay still. Rosie and her sisters had dug graves in their pet cemetery on the hill.

Predeceasing the kittens was a koura, a freshwater crayfish, found in the creek, unable to survive in a kerosene bucket. Next to that spot was a small trench, dug just that summer, holding the remains of a large dragonfly that had fulfilled its ephemeral destiny. Then there were the three kingfisher fledglings. They had thrived in their hand-reared human environment until the boy next door fed them each a large green gooseberry.

Other small bodies had accumulated over the years. It was of some comfort to the girls to ceremonially commit their deceased, with prayer book and shovel, to a shallow grave on the small knoll.

But a grandmother was different. A grandmother has no beginning for her grandchildren and should have no end. And now there was an end. True, she had been ill for what seemed like ages. There had been visits to her bedside—the first unnatural thing, seeing her grandmother being attended to. For Nan was busy: an organizer, a provider, a baker of fruit cakes. As she lay in bed, grandfather hovered nearby, entirely superfluous.

Then distant and hitherto unknown relatives visited, with whispered consultations among the adults. Rosie saw the china cabinet gradually depleted of this or that object of worth. There were no explanations, no acknowledgment of the disappearances, just the absence of old familiar treasures, a jarring end to the order of things.

Rosie had asked, "Where are the blue cups with Japanese paintings on them?" only to be met with a look of silent reproach. There were visits from the doctor with his medical bag, followed by more hushed conversations which, try as she might, she could not decode. And now today the finality of Nan's death gave Rosie much to ponder.

As the day of the funeral progressed a studio photographer was hired to record the occasion. It was every bit as thrilling as a wedding portrait, with the tallest in the middle, the shorter on the ends and the three girls in front. Never had Rosie felt so important. She pushed her hair into her beret and stood tall. Pulling her jumper down over the bodice of her tartan pleated skirt she smiled widely to the command of the photographer.

And the food! It was more sumptuous than the biggest Women's Division Afternoon Tea. With their mother busy, there was no forbidding of second or even third helpings. The girls ate to the extent of their desires, and beyond.

Father had thankfully ceased crying. Mother poured tea, washed dishes, passed around plates of sausage rolls, queen cakes, thin slices of bread and butter, lamingtons and scones. The sponges were the best, all piled high with cream on top.

Rosie concluded that this was the best day in her entire life. Her last best day had been when she went to Rotorua, but this would be so much more boast-worthy at school. The food alone would impress her classmates, and having seen a dead person would raise her status far above the ranks of the lowly.

She pondered some questions on this auspicious day. Her grandmother drove a large Chevrolet. What would grandfather do now? He couldn't drive. Indeed, so nervous a passenger was he that Rosie had seen him leap out of the moving car after berating Nan for perceived near-collisions, preferring to walk to town. How would the family ever again enjoy junket with magical slithers of ice in it, made in Nan's fridge? A sense of desolation came upon her along with the fear that her father might start crying again.

Later that night, after the family made the long journey home and the girls weary, but jubilant, were tucked into their beds, Rosie reflected on the day. She considered that junket made without a fridge tasted reasonably good, especially if a lot of nutmeg was sprinkled on top. And her father showed no sign of further tears. Yes, it had been a strange but good death and an even better funeral.

Farm Life & Death

George Bernard Shaw famously said that "New Zealand's economy floats on a river of blood." I, at the tender age of twelve, saw one of the contributing rivulets when our school visited the Waitara Freezing Works.

Historic photo of the Waitara Freezing Works

Waitara, with its large Maori population, was a Freezing Works town. We always knew when we were approaching Waitara because of the smell of cooking meat meal (rendered meat and bones).

It hung over the town, an all-pervading meaty, cooking-in-the-kitchen sort of smell. Weather prognostications were made from the direction of the smell. Smell coming in from the sea meant it would rain, smell wafting toward the sea, weather fine.

Blood, waste, and effluent were discharged from the Works into the Waitara River, which often ran red after a shift. Everyone knew you could catch the biggest snapper fish in the tidal river just below the Works. In today's heightened environmental awareness, the state of the river and its smell wouldn't be tolerated, but in those times they were comfortable reminders of who we were, where we were, and an assurance of our continued livelihood on the family farm.

The hooter (siren) announced to every resident and worker the end of shifts and noon time. When we went shopping in Waitara our activities were organised around that hooter. Dad would say, "When the hooter goes, come back to the car."

And so—to the Freezing Works one day for our school visit. Our guide apologized that we had arrived too late to witness the actual slaughtering for the morning. I recall the mute terror in the eyes of penned beasts, awaiting their end, as they smelled the fear and death of those slaughtered before them.

We were taken to the conveyor belts where upended animals on their continuum of death moved slowly along for lines of expert Maori butchers to wield their long and wicked blades. Quicker than our eyes could follow, these men whipped out kidneys and livers: hydatid (tapeworm) infested in one direction, clear organs in another.

Historic photo of the Waitara Freezing Works. This was the assembly line that we school children observed up close.

Disembowelling was done with an economy of movement. Two or three lightening slashes had the entrails slurping, still steaming with the fetid warmth of recent living, into yet another moving receptacle. The intestinal stench filled our nostrils as we stepped our way through the congealed blood on the floor.

There was no waste, as tight grooves drained the sloping walkway into more major flows, channelling the blood into large vats.

Out of vast chilled chambers, dangling matured carcasses flowed unceasingly at a measured pace. This enabled men with electrical saws just enough time to hack and stack large segments of beast on to another conveyor belt. The spilt portions flowed along to skilled boners, again with desperately sharp curved knives, allowing them a moment or two for adroitly removing sundry bones.

The large, limp flaps of flesh then made their way to a long line of women. The women wore hairnets and their white gumboots were smeared with blood. With the finesse of long practice they rolled, cut, trimmed, slapped and packed, transforming the amorphous slabs into respectable roasts and steaks.

The offcuts were thrown into an ever-hungry and moving mouth. This led us to where our noses detected new and pungent odours, something was-cooking. Meat meal, an important by-product, was brewing in vast steamers, bones, scraps, offal, and blood. There was no waste. (At home, we fed our chooks meat meal. When no one was looking, I sometimes scooped a little out to eat, as I stirred warm water into the meal.)

The sausage making enthralled me. Intestinal casings were washed in huge cauldrons, the contents bouncing and bubbling around as if there were some sinister current endowing life to this cadaverous, blue-grey mass. Then threaded on to long pulleys, the endless ribbons were doused with a variety of saline and disinfecting solutions. Looking paler and cleaner each time they emerged, these were threaded on the long pulleys. Some were wound on vast reels for transport and export, and others made their way to the sausage-making kitchen.

Maori worker slicing offcuts at the Waitara Freezing Works.

The fate of hides was a stunning revelation. The slithering

flesh-peeled skins had perhaps the most vile of outcomes. They were sprayed, drenched, then dunked into sulphurous baths of evil smelling chrome-coloured liquid. This was truly a house of horrors.

It appeared that the lowliest of workers attended the hides. Protected with large leather aprons, and gloves to their armpits, they doused, rinsed, rolled and stacked piles of skins, feet high. It was a relief to get out of the area and to be able to gasp lungfuls of fresh air. It took me some time to connect my old black shoes with these poor tortured parts of an animal.

I remember the collection of fat, much of it rendered in giant vats, heated to become tallow, for export and candles. This had significance for me as our family still used candles as the main source of light. Electricity was not yet available in our valley. From that day, burning a candle held a whole new raft of understandings for me. I used to think, *I am burning a bullock. I wonder if it hurt him to get killed. I wonder if he was from our farm and has come back to make light for us.*

I used to ponder the process of grass becoming a bullock, bullock becoming a candle and a candle burning into nothing. *Where had the poor animal gone?* I worried.

I was a farm kid and accustomed to animal death. This however was death on a commercial scale, death for profit; the animals weren't old, sick, or injured. No, here was planned and organized massacre of the young and the healthy, and the place stank. It was an appalling spectacle with an overpowering animal gut stench. It seemed a terrible ignominy for animals with big gentle dark eyes and film star eyelashes. They were animals we had often hand reared, named, and loved nearly as much as our siblings.

I was never one for sausages after that visit. However I was aware that our farm contributed generously to the slaughter schedules of the Freezing Works. And there was no other way for our family to be in the world. Dad had been a farmer all his days. Skins, wool, sausage casings, sides of mutton, roasts of beef, and bags of meat meal were a fact of life—for us and thousands more New Zealanders.

With the passage of time, I allowed myself to eat mince and sausages again, and I had always known and accepted Dad slaughtering a sheep for our almost constant menu of mutton. Of course he never allowed his children to be present at the demise of the chosen animal. That was strictly 'men's business'. Thank you, Dad.

Time Warp

At twelve years and four months Rosie was uprooted from her home in the valley and transplanted to a boarding school run in the strict and stern Presbyterian tradition.

Rosie's introduction to both the boarding establishment and the large school for girls was a double agony. Getting sized and fitted up for uniform, house dress and house shoes was a shock. She scrunched her toes into the largest size shoes, which were pronounced a perfect fit by Matron, who bristled in a huge starched white veil, red cape and white nurse's uniform.

"Don't worry," Matron urged, "one size more or less fits all."

The blue serge button-to-the-neck dress prickled her neck unbearably. The gym tunic stuffed Rosie to the north and south of the tie belt. She silently gasped at the mirror's revelation of herself in the formal dress to be worn to church each week. Ignoring Rosie's grimace, Matron declared her suitably attired. Uniformity and conformity were all important, as Rosie would soon discover.

Dormitory life was ruthless. The strong overpowered the weak, the prefects overpowered the strong, the sub-matrons ruled over the prefects and Matron reigned as Supreme Being over all.

Homesickness, criticism of the Headmistress and folding of arms were expressly forbidden. The students were expected to be on time, in correct uniform, and in the right place at all times.

The first day was 'jam jar day'. All new girls had to queue at the infirmary to present a conspicuously generous specimen of urine, while the senior girls gloated and ridiculed. It was difficult to imagine who would test these specimens for hidden diseases, but the procedure was obviously important to some governing body. After uniform inspection by one of the sub-matrons, correctly dressed girls could proceed to the school. Those incorrectly dressed were allocated a variety of penalties doled out by the prefects.

Finding her way around the school was daunting for Rosie. And dangerous. She innocently strayed to an out-of-bounds area at the front formal entrance. Its high imposing post-Victorian façade was not unlike the famous French Arc De Triomphe in Paris.

Rosie was promptly accosted by a prefect, chastised and given a page of Shakespeare to be memorised for the next day. The average twelve year old doesn't readily understand King Lear and reeling off a page seemed an impossibility. Reporting the next day, Rosie erred in some of the lines. Now there were two pages to be learnt by the following day.

Rosie's thirty-five classmates were all similarly stowed into identical 'gym' tunics, worn over a long sleeved white shirt with a silver and navy neck tie, making it difficult for her to distinguish one student from the other for some weeks. These so called 'gym' tunics, worn in high schools all over New Zealand, were the regular uniform and oddly, not for doing gym. As in the dormitory, the strong dominated in the classroom and the hesitant or shy were ridiculed. Academic prowess was the currency for status and acceptance. Rosie was low in such currency. Very low.

After some weeks there was one girl, Janice, who smiled at her, and in fact smiled several times at her. Here was an island in a sea of storms, a lifebelt, and a safe harbour. Rosie swam desperately, as one drowning, towards Janice. Janice invited her to drink a bottle of school milk at the milk station at interval. As much as Rosie loathed school milk, inevitably tainted by sunlight, she eagerly drained her bottle. Thus was born a friendship. It was a tenuous birth, nothing dramatic or instantaneous but rather the nervous edging together of two girls. Janice, a day-girl or in the vernacular of the boarders, a 'day-bug', returned to her family at the end of each day.

For Rosie it was the letters from home that held the promise of seeing her beloved family in the Valley at the Easter break. Until this time, she must hold on for grim death. On the journey home for this holiday Rosie, excited as she was, appreciated things she had never thought about until now—the smell of dampness when she wound down the car windows, the swish of the muddy gravel road, and the presence of her little sisters.

After the Easter break, the next hotly anticipated event was Free Sunday, when boarders could visit nearby friends or family for the day, providing a formal letter of arrangement was submitted to the Matron. Janice's mother sent a note inviting Rosie to their home, outlining the time they would pick her up and return her to the boarding hostel.

The two friends with heads together, straws drawing up the slightly rancid milk, planned each moment of the promised day's outing. Free Sunday finally arrived, with Rosie out of bed and racing for an early shower before the water cooled. Hair slicked down, anchored with a large hairclip and dressed in the required costume, Rosie hopped up and down waiting for Janice, who eventually arrived with her parents and younger brother.

At a local park, Janice's father bought bountiful fourpenny ice-creams for all. After licking and strolling, they returned home to a roast meal. Afternoon tea followed all too soon. Polite conversation, some relaxed listening to the radio and a good deal of giggling by the girls brought this most pleasant day to its close.

That night as she snuggled into her dormitory bunk, Rosie decided that she should invite Janice to stay on the farm in the upcoming May holidays. She would show her guest some of her favourite spots in the bush. Perhaps they could go to ping-pong on Saturday night. And the kittens—there would doubtless be one for Janice to keep. Reflection turned to dreaming, until dreams were interrupted by the insistent morning bell, which sawed its strident tones into Rosie's sleep.

At the milk stand the following day, Rosie and Janice relived the day before where the ice-creams became huge, the roast meal fit for a king, and the park a paradise.

Somewhere between paradise and the interval bell, Rosie found herself inviting Janice to visit at the farm. It was now Rosie's opportunity to show largesse. They would sleep in the same room. Together they could search for the wily old house cow and the country girl would show the town girl how to milk it. She would teach her the trick of squirting milk straight into cat's mouths.

When she heard the plans, Janice quivered with excitement and anticipation. She could think of nothing she would rather do. She was positive her parents would let her have a kitten. Maybe two.

The daily planning proceeded, until Rosie could no longer ignore a nagging unease. She tried to push her disquiet away, applying herself with unusual diligence to her assignments each evening. Although strictly forbidden, Rosie was rather given to writing a letter home under the guise of essay writing when the sub-matrons supervised the evening compulsory two-hour homework session.

She later tore out the page from her exercise book

knowing the family back home would not be critical of her choice of stationery.

On Friday night however, when there was no homework, Rosie finally allowed the fretful feeling to take shape, and soon that feeling took on the shape of a candle. That was it, the lights. How could she have been so dumb? How could she ever admit to Janice the humiliating truth? That her family used candles—when they went to bed, to walk up the pathway with its ridiculous steps and to go to the outside lavatory.

Rosie had her own favourite chipped white enamel candleholder, which she propped up so she could read in bed each night, handy for quickly blowing out when she heard her mother's footsteps. But she could never admit these things to Janice. What would Janice think about the lighting of the two gaslights in the kitchen and sitting room each evening?

There were double gas cylinders which exuded a terrible gassy stink and hissed ominously when connecting up. Her father shouted instructions and warnings, ordering the family to stand back as their hero and rescuer aligned the tap and screwed on the gas cylinder.

Then with more shouted instructions he stood on a chair, turned the tap on, struck up a match and coaxed the delicate mesh mantle into life, lighting up the sitting room. When it glowed with its cold small light and the smell had dissipated, Rosie always sighed with relief.

There was something inherently dangerous about these rituals. And something shameful with her father's shouting and admonitions to "Stand back" or "Mind out" or "Where are the matches?"

She remembered when her big sister had ended the mantle's ephemeral life by piercing it with the lighted match. There had been a good deal of shouting and blaming then.

No, Janice must not see how primitive, how old-fashioned her family was. Janice could not come and visit the Valley. Rosie was relieved to make this decision, ending the discomfit that had settled upon her like a cold valley fog.

A letter from home arrived the next morning that quite disconcerted Rosie and blew her plans awry.

The family wrote about the cats, and picking field mushrooms, the sort of news that made her long for the May holidays.

Then at the end, a short sentence saying that her mother had written to Janice's parents regarding the holiday. Rosie, who had just struggled through a Latin translation of King Canute, knew with sickening certainty that Janice's visit was now as unstoppable as the tide.

Monday's rendezvous amongst the milk crates found Janice with growing relish for her upcoming farm experience. Rosie, with fast diminishing enthusiasm, could barely speak. As the bell rang, Rosie felt it was tolling the inevitable arrival of her mother's letter in Janice's letterbox.

That night, Rosie stayed awake wracked by her worry and how she must tell Janice the truth. The next morning at the milk station it was time to launch her declaration. In a voice that faltered to an almost whisper she laid bare her secret. "We don't have electric lights or ... anything electric." Now she could let it go.

"How does your mother cook?" Janice asked incredulously. "How do you see at night? How...?"

But when Janice heard about the candles, she was ecstatic. "Candles! How utterly romantic!" she enthused. "That would be just like the olden days. I would so love to go to bed with a candle!"

Rosie was stunned with surprise, which timidly grew to relief and then galloped to pleasure. Her world spun with the wonderful turn of events. She grinned at Janice, causing Janice to observe this was only the fourth time she'd ever seen Rosie looking happy.

"Happy?" exclaimed Rosie, "this has been the best year of my life so far!"

Pants on fire

High school was over for the year and Rosie was home at last with her family. Books packed away, she was now free to wander the beloved hills she had seen so little of during the past school year.

But Rosie was not enjoying the early summer coolness. The little sisters she had so long eulogised and pined for, now seemed familiar and irksome. She saw how workworn her mother was and rediscovered the ever-constant toil necessary to keep the farm running smoothly. Rosie felt that her father's every glance held a question, even though he was a mild-mannered adoring parent. The question hanging in the air pained Rosie, and she awoke every day with a heavy dread. As she listened for the cream mail lorry each morning Rosie endured a sort of death until the mail was brought from the letterbox and duly opened by her father. But each day had not brought the news Rosie dreaded.

Another day of what should have been summer delight—swimming in the creek, mustering, haymaking, rounding up and milking the old red house-cow, stroking all the cats and choosing names for the newest litter of kittens. All these activities Rosie embraced with a desperate fervour. Choosing not to remember a year of indifferent studentship, she was home at last, safe, loved, cherished and alas, ashamed.

For Rosie had done wrong, very wrong. It had to do

with French and Latin. Rosie, the little brumby from the hills had not taken kindly to being tethered and trained. Each list of vocab to be learned by heart wilted her carefree spirit. Parsing Latin verbs was as a painfully tight sirloin strap and each French translation was a high brush hurdle. The hills' brumby had pawed and snorted with dismay at the rigours of academia and had cantered off in quite the opposite direction.

Rosie remembered all too clearly when and where her moral decline had taken root. When she was home for the Easter break. Family friends, four farms below them in the valley, were visiting for a Sunday roast when that awkward question was asked: "How are you doing with your French, Rosie?"

Stifling an involuntary gasp, Rosie managed to look squarely at Mrs Steed and say "Very well, thank you." She remembered the look of adoration from her father. If only he had known that her last French test yielded her three marks out of twenty, and a detention.

Her father had spoken up proudly, "Rosie's learning Latin too, you know."

Another probing query from Mrs Steed about that state of affairs.

"Yes, I'm doing even better in Latin than in French," Rosie had lied. Thankfully she was shielded from further interrogation by Mr Steed pontificating, "Latin is a dead language."

If only, thought Rosie.

August holidays arrived with the little brumby still in a state of revolt. Now there were questions from Rosie's parents. There seemed to be some urgency and concern in their rather direct enquiries, which invited equally direct answers. Drowning in her sinful past, she felt there was no option but to placate their concerns with ready assurances that all was well with French and Latin. So well, that she had topped her class in French and was in line for winning the Latin cup, for Third Form. How painfully proud were her parents. And how painfully miserable was Rosie.

And now with the year behind her, Rosie's world went by in slow motion as she waited for her report to arrive in the mail any day now. A small part of her would be relieved to disentangle herself from the deceit but the biggest part would be mortified when the truth about the dreaded languages would be out. What would her parents do? Would they tell Mr and Mrs Steed? Would they ever feel proud of her again? Would they even still love her?

Rosie turned in her bed, facing the wall. She blinked away the tears as she heard the roar of the cream lorry with its bundle of mail, pulling in to their gate.

The Interview

I have left school and applied for a job that sounds promising: a government cadetship in administration. There it is: my letter, with its official letterhead. I have an interview with the manager of the State Advances, a housing finance agency.

The thought of being a working girl, earning money, and leaving behind my school gym tunic is hugely appealing to this sixteen-year-old. After considering the two other options available to girls leaving school in the mid 1950s, nursing or teaching, my choice is office work. I see myself as one of those busty, tight-skirted secretaries, efficient and film-star attractive. It can surely be only a matter of time.

Excitement surges through the gully. Neighbours inquire and are informed. The manual phone is rung with a flourish as the bush telegraph buzzes: *Did you know that Sunny is going for a job?* I gaze down benevolently at my two younger sisters thinking how soon I'll be leaving them and living in town. My father clucks with pride as my mother works out what will be worn to the interview.

It is early autumn and coolish, so my grey overcoat will be just the thing. On reflection I now see it as the shape and colour of a cow cover, with its coarse wool and undefined cut. In those heady times, however, it was my ideal of what was fashionable and likely to persuade a manager to employ me. More news for the bush telegraph:

She's going to wear her grey coat and you should see the grey high-heeled shoes she has bought! I practice walking without wobbling in my newly acquired footwear. "Point your toes OUT!" Mum prompts. More wobbling. Now a little more confident, I strut out before my adoring family, parading in the coat as well.

"Hands out of your pockets," admonishes Mum.

I don't recall what I wore under the coat. In all probability a homemade skirt and some sort of jumper. Memory, however, has preserved the memory of the hat. Silk, velvet, bright cherry pink with a soft slouchy brim. Pulled down respectfully it should create the demure, work-like stance of a maiden at an interview. I experiment with lipstick, which makes my thin lips look uncharacteristically livid. "No," Mum says firmly, "you don't need to look like a harlot". No lipstick. I am allowed to use her *Evening in Paris* perfume, dabbing my neck and wrists from the tiny midnight blue bottle. This is privilege. I am on the cusp of real womanhood, intoxicating in its possibilities.

I stage a dress rehearsal for the nearest neighbours, who are wowed to silence by my air of grownupness and my perfume. Queen Bee, Princess, Fairy on the Christmas tree, Film Star—I am all of these as I float through the next weeks of unbridled expectation. There is a trip to town to make last arrangements, buy new stockings and an undergarment of torture known as 'easies", required to ensure utter slimness. I slide on the elasticated girdle, attach stockings to the suspender clips and behold I have no observable stomach or bottom. It matters not that after I eat a meal while wearing the garment I endure hours of agony as my pubescent innards struggle to do their digestive duties, in spite of the fearful constriction.

And so to the Day of Days. Up extra early, telephone line ringing hotly, then into the car for the fateful journey.

The cream lorry wends its way up our gully, spewing forth its cargo of empty cream cans, groceries, bread and mail, at each cowshed, replenishing itself with full cans of milk cream.

Neighbours stand at their gates and wave encouragement as my proud parents drive me to the city. I smell the cool dampness of the gully, hear the mud swish under our tyres, and think, *No more of this for me.* The allure of city life beckons me and I am ready: job, working woman, money.

World, here I come!

Red Dress

Rosie had tried the Life of the Office Girl and decided it to be lacking so she decided to become a teacher.

The process was extraordinarily easy. A phone call, a brief interview with a couple of bored looking interviewers and a written acceptance all occurred within a month. With much relief and a surge of excitement she handed in her notice and resolutely left the clerical world behind.

The Training College stipend was meagre, leaving Rosie with uncomfortable decisions concerning how to survive on such a lowly income. The bus fare from where she boarded to the college used up precious shillings each day. For a country girl there was a workable solution. She would walk the miles to the college except for wet or foggy days when she used the luxury of a bus ride. College was a full social life for Rosie, who relished all the comings and goings of learning to be a teacher.

The area was renowned for its foggy winters, harsh frosts and rain that pelted down, winter and summer. As the year progressed Rosie shivered. At great expense she bought a bottle green corduroy jacket on time payment, coaxed her landlady to dole out another blanket, and did her assignments tucked up in bed, jacket around her shoulders, feet on a hot water bottle, in order to keep out the penetrating dampness and cold.

About the middle of the year, Rosie was invited to a church social. Given to resourceful and practical ideas she decided to sew herself a red dress. Having seen one in a glossy magazine some time ago Rosie wanted desperately to have such a garment. Red would be a cheerful enough colour for any social occasion, and if the material was warm, she would be able to leave the corduroy jacket at home for the evening in question.

Never for a moment did she consider any other colour. Ever since she could remember she'd been dressed in red. Her mother had decided that was Rosie's colour, whereas her next youngest sister was pre-ordained for blue. Rosie had sometimes wondered how she might look, if one day she too could wear something blue. Or pink. But her mother had warned her off pink. "Light colours show the dirt," proclaimed her practical parent, whereas red never did. And, as her mother explained, "blue wouldn't suit you at all, because you have brown eyes." Blue was the rightful domain of those, like her next youngest sister, who had eyes to match.

With this wisdom Rosie saved her bus shillings until she had enough money to finally look for some red fabric. There it was in the old Drapers Shop with the creaky wooden floor, a bolt of bright cherry-red pure-wool coating material. For these were the times, and this was the town where every self-respecting woman owned a winter coat, except of course Rosie, with her corduroy jacket.

Excitedly, she turned the pages of the Butterick pattern book, until she saw just the version of a dress she'd dreamed of wearing. Flared skirt, nipped in and belted at the waist, long sleeves with cuffs, a high mandarin collar and front opening. Rosie could see herself swept along the dance floor, skirt a-swirling, in her high heels with all eyes upon her.

In a glow of anticipation, Rosie hardly felt the cold as she laid out pattern pieces on the floor of her bedroom, pinning them onto the red fabric. It would hardly matter if the front panels of the skirt could not be cut on the cross, as the material seemed not to have a grain, and after all, nobody would compare the back of the dress with the front, at the same time. Then came the arduous task of cutting out.

Rosie had only a pair of household scissors, which were hardly up to the task of munching through a double layer of woollen coating. There were gashes in the fabric, as she strove to cut, her tortured knuckles showing white with the pressure.

Eventually every last piece was cut and checked off the list; inside facings, double collar pieces, cuffs, bodice, skirt, sleeves and belt. Well satisfied with her evening's achievement, Rosie climbed into bed, rubbing away the pain in her fingers. She caressed her hot water bottle, imagining it to be some handsome boy at the church social, and fell asleep sewing and dancing simultaneously.

For the next week assignments gave way to the construction of the red dress. Rosie's second-hand sewing machine that started with a spray of sparks and acrid electrical fumes, was nevertheless reliable and up to the task of sewing 2 layers of coating fabric. However when collar *and* facing *and* bodice all had to come together, the sewing machine belched fumes and came to a stall at four layers of the substantial fabric. But Rosie was not to be beaten by this set-back. With determination borne of desperation, she winched the wheel around, causing the needle to take large greedy stitches. At least they were on the inside of the dress, and not be seen. Gradually, painfully, the dress took form. Putting in the side zip was an ordeal. Folding the red material to sit on each side of the zip, was nigh impossible. Each stitch was achieved by Rosie coaxing the wheel over the hillocks of fabric. After all, she rationalised, if she held her arm over her left side, no-one would notice irregularities in the zip area.

Finally, it was stitched sufficiently to try on. With heart racing, Rosie pulled it impatiently over her head, jamming the zip together and pulling the high collar to one side, in an effort to straighten the dress.

The belt was her next challenge. She was able to sew the required tube, but to turn it inside out and pull it through on the right side of itself proved quite impossible. After conceding defeat, she thought of a satisfactory solution. She would buy a belt. A few more days of walking, to save her shillings, found Rosie choosing a wide black belt. Very wide and very fashionable. That would match her black flat shoes, and it would serve the useful function of covering the whole of the waistline, which was somewhat bulky and irregular.

The mandarin collar was slightly off-centre and itched her neck. But Rosie knew what every girl knows; comfort comes a distant second to looks.

The landlady, invited to view Rosie in the red dress, stood back and measured her words carefully. "Hmm, well it will certainly keep you warm" was the nearest to a compliment that could be elicited from that worthy woman, who was rather spare with praise at the best of times.

It was a disappointment to Rosie that the dress didn't have much lift in the skirt, when she twirled in front of the mirror. Perhaps the belt should be tighter she thought. Drawing in her breath, she winched the buckle up another notch, in the same way she was used to tightening the surcingle on her old horse Molly.

Blind in one eye, Molly compensated for her lack of sight with much cunning. She would distend her girth, when being saddled up, then trot off allowing her belly to resume its natural circumference, thus achieving a deliciously loose saddle. Startling, if approached on her blind side, Molly had learned to startle whichever side she was mounted on, if she sensed the rider was inexperienced and young. But this was a high and heady life for Rosie, far removed from her Home in the Valley and the horses.

The night of the church social, the fog settled damp and bleak, its icy breath penetrating every part of Rosie's world. A pang of gratitude throbbed within her, for the warmth of the sturdy red dress. There was no budget for high heels but her flat shoes polished up well with her father's cornflour and spit method. The 'surcingle' was taken in yet another notch, leaving Rosie straining for breath, tensed and ready for the impending social.

Entering the church hall, she was disconcerted to see the other girls in summer-weight fantastically frilled dresses and skirts, wearing nothing more than a cardigan over their shoulders. How could this be so, in the middle of winter? Rosie could imagine her mother cautioning those foolhardy girls about the likelihood of chest colds and worse.

Friends greeting friends, had cause to look in the direction of Rosie and her red coating dress, for such is the nature of red. It's the stop signal—The synonym for danger, the symbol of sin, the colour for bullfights. There were significant glances from one surprised friend to another. Someone, lacking in manners, stifled a guffaw. Others endowed with more sensitivity eyed that person and silenced her with their wordless indignation.

Settling herself next to the kindly minister's wife Rosie exchanged pleasantries as she waited for the dancing to begin. Those who felt the need to turn for a better view of the dress were greeted by the minister's wife giving a cheery wave, disconcerting them and directing their eyes to a more proper focus.

Brazen and brash Lola Prettimouse felt the need to approach Rosie, saying "I like your dress. Did you sew it yourself?" The Minister's wife using the language of her eyes sent Miss Prettimouse retreating to the other side of the church hall.

Then the music started. Piped through the hall's sound system it was something of a shock to Rosie, who'd been used to the old Returned Services Hall back in the Valley. Paddy O'Reilly belting out the waltzes on the ancient honky tonky piano and Peter Black with his saxophone, compensating for any of the piano's dud keys. At least it had been lively and alive. None of this canned music stuff. Another thing to surprise her mother about.

And another thing to surprise Rosie. These were the dances of Rock and Roll, with their strange and sensuous beat. The cardigan wearers whirled and twirled with partners who knew how to set them spinning. Rosie gasped at the intricate turns with skirts and petticoats flying out till one could catch a fleeting glimpse of lacy knickers. This was a world unknown to Rosie. As she beheld these wonders, her fingers felt the coarse fibre of her dress. Where were the old familiar waltzes, the Gay Gordons, the foxtrots? And where were the invitations for Rosie to dance?

The minister's wife excused herself to search for her husband, who in turn searched for their son, who thus prompted, came to Rosie and asked her to dance.

"I suppose your mother told you to come and ask me for a dance," she muttered.

"Certainly not," said he.

"Well," said she. "I don't know any Rock and Roll."

"Well," said he, pulling her on to the dance floor, "there's no better time to learn."

Rosie saw the pimples on the minister's son's face up close, too close. As he taught her the more basic Rock and Roll routines, Rosie's squeezed abdomen screamed out in revolt, until she had to take the wide black belt out a couple of notches, causing the couple nearest them to snicker as they swung through their routine. "I reckon you know it now," declared the minister's son, leading her off the dance floor.

Rosie sat out the next few dances, mainly because there were no requests for her to dance. By now the surcingle had done its damage and needed desperately to be removed—if only the waistline had been sewed more successfully. Two girls she had sometimes seen in church sidled up to her and asked "Is it true that you come from the country?"

"Yep, same country as you."

This caused the girls to erupt into giggles as they walked off. *It's the dress*, thought Rosie. She felt herself colour as she considered her plight. Determined to sew herself a swirly skirt with petticoats, Rosie calculated she'd have to walk to college every day for seven and a half weeks to save up for the materials. She already had a pair of lacy knickers and her flat black shoes would be alright. Definitely no belt next time.

Suppertime was a welcome punctuation to the evening. The long trestle tables in the supper room were laden with cream sponges, chocolate cakes, pikelets, stuffed eggs, lamingtons, asparagus rolls, thickly buttered scones and steaming sausage rolls—none of which Rosie could eat, owing to restrictions of the belt with its resulting agony of the abdomen. She sipped at a cup of tea and as soon as was socially acceptable, slipped away to the toilets, where she sat and removed the belt for a minute or two of sweet relief.

The door creaked as the Minister's wife called "You alright Rosie? The dancing will be starting again soon."

Rosie answered, "Yes thank you Mrs Lovejoy. Just coming," and with a tightening of the belt and a flush of the toilet she emerged. "Actually I think I should be going home now, because the last bus comes in about 10 minutes."

The minister's wife seemed to understand and invited Rosie to come to tea the next Sunday night.

As Rosie waited at the bus stop, mouthing steamy circles into the night air, a car pulled up, a window wound down and someone called out, "Hi Rosie, want a lift?"

Peering into the car, she saw the driver was Kenny, a mature age student teacher, in her section. "Yes please, but are you going in my direction?"

"I need to take a folio of horseracing results to the local radio station and if you want to come for the ride, I can drop you home after that."

Rosie felt she could have kissed him, so grateful was she for this improved ending to the evening. Of course she wouldn't really do any kissing, but how nice to brag to her chums on Monday morning that THE Kenny had driven her home.

During the drive across town, Rosie learned he was employed by the local radio station to report and collect race results for broadcasting. And Kenny learned that Rosie was a keen exponent of Rock and Roll and had danced the night away at the Church Social, sadly having to come home because of the last bus.

And when Kenny said he liked the red dress, Rosie felt he really meant it. More wondrous things to tell her mother...

After thanking him for the lift, she tiptoed inside, and was soon tucked up in bed with her hot water bottle. Life, thought Rosie, was very good.

Photos From Our Album

The Weed in The Garden

The weed in the garden
makes the rose seem so sweet
The ache of the journey
gives strength to the feet.

The pain of the nettles
brings food to the soil
The death of old forests
yields up its good oil.

But the weed in the garden
has something to say
For we need thorns and thistles
in our lives day to day.

The cold of the winter
shares the warmth of the fire
The heart that is broken
brims full with desire.

The cry of a baby
calls forth tender love.
The mire down below
grows the lilies above.

But the weed in the garden
has something to say.
For we need thorns and thistles
in our lives day to day.

Acknowledgements

Like the apex of a triangle my collection of stories sits atop a raft of people, who have contributed in many and various ways to the birthing of *Taranaki Sunshine*. It has proved to be a slow and sometimes painful birth, mainly because of my procrastinations, but ultimately worth everyone's effort.

To Roslyn Bullas McKay, my special thanks for her labour of love, in publishing my blog thus encouraging me to put my childhood tales to pen and paper. Also to Roslyn my everlasting thanks for editing the stories to a book-worthy standard.

My heartfelt thanks to Mary Gabb, lifetime friend, motivator and fan of my stories. She has proved that holding a carrot to the donkey is not nearly as effective as vigorously prodding it from the rear with occasional threats and admonishments!

To Linda Brooks, I am entirely grateful for her many hours of creating the book and organising it's publishing, and for her persistent encouragement.

I thank my sister Betsey Thomson for remembering our childhood—often more accurately than I. And for her enjoyment and corrections of remembered or misremembered details.

To other family members and friends who come under the banner of prodders, urgers and appreciators, I thank you with much affection.

www.ingramcontent.com/pod-product-compliance
Lightning Source LLC
Chambersburg PA
CBHW031421290426
44110CB00011B/477